P

"[Striner] engages in a fair-minded and perceptive parsing of Lincoln's words regarding race, starting with the Peoria speech. He also discusses Lincoln's policies to end slavery, such as his unwillingness, after he was elected in 1860, to compromise with the South to allow slavery to expand into the territories; his unwillingness, as the North grew war-weary, to end the war with slavery intact; and his behind-the-scenes efforts to have Louisiana and Tennessee restored to the Union without slavery."

—**Henry Cohen**, *The Federal Lawyer*

"Washington College history professor Richard Striner weighs the evidence and concludes that, not only was Lincoln free of racial bias, but he also was a political genius willing to deceive his opponents about his racial attitudes to further the cause of human rights."

—*Star Democrat*

"Terse, unflinching, and cogent. Striner forthrightly vindicates Lincoln from the stigma of racism through a close textual analysis of his most controversial speeches and by careful attention to their political context. He persuasively shows how Lincoln consistently employed evasive and conditional language to disarm the racial pandering of his opponent and the recalcitrant fears of his audience. While making seemingly important concessions to the inflexible racial prejudice of his audience, Lincoln nonetheless subtly upheld core egalitarian principles. As a lawyer, Lincoln used this strategy of conceding a narrow point while upholding a more fundamental principle to great effect. As a statesman, his use of this same strategy was at once necessary and masterful: it enabled him to survive politically while maintaining the viability of the antislavery cause in the racist state of Illinois and throughout the Union. Far from being a white supremacist, then, Lincoln was a master politician whose political craft was indispensable in advancing equality and black freedom against the prevailing climate of white supremacy. This book is a must-read for anyone interested in the provocative yet perilous question of Lincoln and race."

—**Joseph R. Fornieri**, author of
Abraham Lincoln, Philosopher Statesman

"Abraham Lincoln was both a pragmatic politician seeking office and the most profound moral philosopher ever to occupy the presidency. The contradictions between the two roles were enormous, leaving in their wake apparently irreconcilable statements about the most emotional issue of his day, racial equality. Richard Striner's impressive exercise in decoding Lincoln's rhetoric takes us as far as one can go in discovering the Great Emancipator's bedrock opinion."

—**Alonzo L. Hamby**, author of *For the Survival of Democracy: Franklin Roosevelt and the World Crisis of the 1930s*

CONCISE
LINCOLN
LIBRARY

—

EDITED BY RICHARD W. ETULAIN,
SARA VAUGHN GABBARD, AND
SYLVIA FRANK RODRIGUE

RICHARD STRINER

Lincoln and Race

Southern Illinois University Press
Carbondale

Southern Illinois University Press
www.siupress.com

Copyright © 2012, 2022 by the Board of Trustees,
Southern Illinois University
All rights reserved. Cloth edition 2012.
Paperback edition 2022.
Printed in the United States of America

25 24 23 22   4 3 2 1

The Concise Lincoln Library has been made possible
in part through a generous donation by the Leland E.
and LaRita R. Boren Trust.

Cover illustration adapted from a painting by
Wendy Allen

The Library of Congress has catalogued the 2012
hardcover and ebook editions as follows:
ISBN 978-0-8093-3077-5 (cloth)
ISBN 978-0-8093-3087-2 (ebook)

Library of Congress Cataloging-in-Publication Data
Names: Striner, Richard, 1950– author.
Title: Lincoln and race / Richard Striner.
Identifiers: LCCN 2022029107 | ISBN
9780809338900 (paperback)
Subjects: LCSH: Lincoln, Abraham, 1809-1865—
Political and social views. | Lincoln, Abraham,
1809–1865—Relations with African Americans. |
]United States—Race relations—History—19th
century. | BISAC: BIOGRAPHY & AUTOBIOGRAPHY /
Presidents & Heads of State | SOCIAL SCIENCE /
Ethnic Studies / American / African American &
Black Studies
Classification: LCC E457.2 .S893 2022 |
DDC 973.7—dc23/eng/20220722
LC record available at https://lccn.loc.
gov/2022029107

Printed on recycled paper ♻

Southern Illinois University System

To my parents, to Sara, and to Sommer

CONTENTS

PREFACE

Perhaps it would be best to begin by explaining my views about "race."

I regard that unfortunate term as a label for patterns in the physical appearance of large population groups within the human species. These patterns are obviously inherited. So are other physical patterns and characteristics that do not play a role in the concept of "race": differences in the overall size and shape of the human body, for instance, that appear in rather random form across the race lines.

I have no idea how much further the patterns of "racial" inheritance may happen to extend beyond the outward features of skin tone, hair texture (and color), and the shape of certain facial features. Some susceptibilities to disease may be higher for certain racial groups, according to the medical literature. But attempts to establish verifiable differences in intellectual capacity or personality tendencies among races have erupted into firestorms of methodological criticism, and rightly so.

What is not at all in doubt in my opinion is the fact that race is too often misused by ideologists who try to infer from these patterns certain qualities of inward character that have no correspondence whatsoever to racial identity in my experience. My preference is to de-emphasize the physical traits of human beings in all public interactions with obvious exceptions. Some physical traits call for special accommodation, as in "handicapped access." Others are assets: models, movie stars, performers, and athletes quite rightly emphasize such physical traits. More problematical, certain comedians—at the cost of emotional and moral ambiguities—use physical traits to get a laugh.

In private interactions, the members of a free society will naturally emphasize physical characteristics in a multitude of ways, some benign—as when physical attraction plays a role in romantic attraction—and some malignant.

I think that all attempts to give a positive emphasis to race are more harmful, on balance, than good. I believe that all physical qualities should play a secondary role in our identities, both as we create these identities for ourselves and as others create them in the course of reacting to us.

In sum, I agree with the views of historian Jacques Barzun, whose classic work *Race: A Study in Modern Superstition* is as valid today as the day when it was published in 1937. As late as 2000, with the publication of *From Dawn to Decadence*, Barzun continued to scorn the concept of race as a "notion," a "dogma," a "fallacy," a snare, and a delusion.[1] I agree with him: the only importance of the physical patterns that people call race is the importance that we, in our cultural and ideological belief systems, attribute to them. Beyond that, the term means . . . nothing.

Race sometimes coincides with certain patterns of culture, as when musical genres like blues or rap are identified with African Americans. But "black music" is nothing more than *culture*. It is surely not an issue of biology.

And one has to remember that our subcultures influence and change one another; they exist in unending give-and-take. "Black" and "white" cultural patterns in America have overlapped in many ways for years. The most important fact is this: vast numbers of blacks and whites exist as unique individuals for whom the issue of race is unimportant.

And I regard these people as heroic. For when it comes to the innermost identity of people, the facts about race should be irrelevant. To say otherwise can lead to monstrosity.

Adolf Hitler's genocide is proof of where the race ideology can lead. Even in the course of our everyday lives, we can sense the absurdities that often unfold as racial doctrine impedes the formation of selfhood, especially in children. Consider the challenge of transracial adoption; the reflections that follow are the thoughts of a teenage girl as recorded in *Beneath the Mask*, a guidebook for therapeutic specialists. Consider the comments of "Alyssa": "I might look Korean, but I see myself as American. People, especially my teachers and kids at school that don't know me, base who I am on my appearance. They think if I look Asian, then I am Asian. They are totally wrong. I get mad that I am always having to explain myself. Also, you know about those stereotypes. Just because I am Asian does not mean I am good at math. I suck at math."[2]

The assertion that race is fundamental to identify has blighted the lives of many people. In nineteenth-century America, the proposition was powerful. Millions of people of African descent had to cope with this notion of race. They had to decide what they thought and what they felt about the notion that their race must determine who they were.

So, too, with all the millions of Americans whose ancestors came from other parts of the world—Americans like Abraham Lincoln. This book seeks to ascertain the influence, if any, that the notion of race might have had for our sixteenth president.

LINCOLN AND RACE

INTRODUCTION

The issue of Lincoln's racial views—essentially the issue of his private racial *feelings*—has been raised ever since his rise to national greatness, when Stephen A. Douglas contended that Abraham Lincoln was a secret "negro lover." Others have contended the reverse: that Lincoln was a racist. One of the most fanatical white supremacists of early-twentieth-century America, U.S. Senator James K. Vardaman of Mississippi (the "Great White Chief"), declared that he and Lincoln saw eye to eye on race.[1] And one of the angriest black detractors of Lincoln in the late twentieth century, journalist Lerone Bennett Jr., insisted that Lincoln was a thoroughgoing racist.[2]

A large scholarly literature has probed this topic down the years.[3] And the debate continues—it will never end—because of one very troublesome fact: Lincoln's documented words on the matter of race can be read in opposite ways. At times he uttered words that sounded racist. Yet, on other occasions he sounded like an enemy of racists. So what is one to make of this evidence?

What is really at issue are the innermost feelings of Lincoln. And emotions can be hard to pin down. Even if a person whose views are in question has committed some feelings to a diary—or to private correspondence—there will always be lingering mysteries. Who could possibly claim that they have navigated all the complexities—the deep mixed feelings, the unconscious travail—within the mind of any human being? The full truth about the feelings of others can in many cases never be known.

Even so, this book will take a definite position on the subject. After examining the most reliable evidence concerning Lincoln's racial attitudes—not only toward African Americans but toward other racial groups, such as Native Americans—*Lincoln and Race* will advance the conclusion that in all probability Lincoln had no racial bias.

In his classic detective yarn *The Thin Man*, Dashiell Hammett concluded with a private conversation between the private eye, Nick Charles, and his clever wife, Nora. After laying out his evidence, Nick asks his wife if she has any doubts about the magnitude of "what we've got." "There seems to be enough of it," she answers, "but it's not very neat." Nick replies, "It takes care of all the angles and I can't think of any other theory that would."

One factor has determined the findings of *Lincoln and Race*: any satisfactory theory should make greater sense than the others. And the theory presented in this book is the *only* way it makes sense—to this historian.[4]

LINCOLN, SLAVERY, AND
RACE: THE PROBLEMS

L incoln did service in the Blackhawk War—an Indian war in Illinois. Did this affect his views about race? One will never know: his unit in the 1832 war never actually fought.

Yet, he had some very interesting encounters. He saw the mutilated victims of Indian massacres and intervened to save the life of a peaceful Indian refugee.[1] These are episodes with racial implications—documented episodes. Perhaps some of them were unimportant in the great scheme of things.

His encounters with African Americans—free and enslaved—whom he met in his early adulthood were very important. He recorded one experience vividly; while travelling aboard an Ohio River steamer in 1841, he saw slaves chained together "like so many fish upon a trot line." He remembered this sight for a great many years, and the memory, he wrote later on, was "a continual torment to me."[2]

Most of the available evidence pertaining to Lincoln's racial views must be drawn from the debate about slavery. And his pre-presidential position on the issue is clear. First, he declared that the enslavement of other human beings was a monstrous evil. Second, he insisted that slavery's extension should be halted; he was a vigorous member of the "Free Soil" movement in American politics. Third, he expressed the hope that slavery's containment would be followed by a program that would phase it out. Fourth, he was a vocal advocate of "colonization"—the idea that freed slaves could be resettled in a foreign land—as a voluntary measure for blacks who found the prospect attractive.

There can be little doubt that Lincoln's antislavery views were sincere. But two facets of his position—his Free Soil principles and his advocacy of colonization—have ambiguous meaning if applied to the issue of race. For the antebellum Free Soil movement—the movement to restrict the spread of slavery and keep it out of western territories—could be equally attractive to bigots and believers in equality. And the colonization movement—the program to "ship blacks out of the country"—was a controversial item before the Civil War; many blacks disagreed about its merits, and so did many whites.

It is best to begin with the issues of the Free Soil movement. Why would American whites who regarded black people as inferior— whites who were content to leave slavery alone where it existed— choose to fight (in "Bleeding Kansas," for instance) to prevent the institution of slavery from spreading to the West? This movement, which affected both parties (the Democrats and Whigs) in the 1840s, must be studied to make sense of the historical events that would follow: the events that would shatter the existing party system, create a new "fusion" party (the Republican Party), and lead to civil war.

At the heart of the matter is a very simple question: why did certain white supremacists hate and abominate slavery?

The first reason was basic: if slavery should spread to the West, it would mean that many *blacks* would be moving to the West, and white Americans who wished to see a whites-only West would regard this idea with revulsion. Illinois provides a perfect illustration of this state of mind. In 1831, the state passed a law that required free blacks who wished to settle in the state to post a $1,000 bond, a prohibitive sum. In 1853, the state constitution was amended to prohibit free blacks from coming there at all. This amendment was endorsed by a thumping two-to-one margin of the voters.[3]

But there were other reasons for antipathy to slavery among many northern white supremacists—reasons that ran just as deep. By the 1840s, many members of the Free Soil movement believed that slavery was (or would be in due time) a threat to themselves. As they watched the operations of slavery, they saw very clearly that the liberties of *whites* were on the wane.

Most slave states had passed some draconian laws to prevent slave rebellions, and these laws curbed a liberty of whites: freedom of speech. Under many of the harsh new "slave codes" enacted in the 1830s, antislavery speech became a felony, a criminal offense.[4] First Amendment protections were irrelevant: according to the language of the First Amendment, only Congress is prohibited from curbing or suppressing free speech. (Only later, in 1925, would the U.S. Supreme Court apply the Bill of Rights to the states in the case of *Gitlow v. New York*.)

Many northerners bristled at the notion that the liberties of whites could be curbed by the southern master class. But then the situation escalated: slavery was shown to be a threat to white jobs as well as white speech. White workers at the Tredegar Iron Works in Richmond, Virginia, tried to go on strike for better hours and wages in 1847. The owner of the factory fired them all and had slaves run the factory instead—*rented* slaves.[5] Here was a new demonstration of the threat to the livelihood of whites that could result if the institution of slavery spread.

The threat of slavery to whites was perceived in stronger terms when certain advocates of slavery wrote that "inferior" *whites* should be enslaved. In his 1854 book *Sociology for the South*, the Virginian George Fitzhugh contended that "some were born with saddles on their backs, and others booted and spurred to ride them, and the riding does them good." "Slavery," he continued, "is the natural and normal condition of the working man, whether white or black."[6]

Small wonder that many northern whites began to loathe slavery, regardless of their views on race: it was a clear and present danger to themselves, to their children, to their future.

These facts demand a careful approach to the Free Soil leadership of Lincoln. Many members of the Free Soil movement were white supremacists, but others harbored no racial bias. Free Soil politics could bend either way when it came to the subject of race. So analysis of Lincoln's Free Soil principles must take this into account.

Now a word about colonization.

Black Americans were deeply divided on the issue. Many were insulted by the notion of "deporting" them; a month after the American Colonization Society was founded in December 1816, some black leaders met at Philadelphia's Bethel Church to revile the new organization.[7] The free black leader Simeon Jocelyn condemned it right away.

But the "back to Africa" theme would resound many times among African Americans. The theme had biblical overtones: an exodus from the cruel house of bondage to the promised land of the Patriarchs could sound providential if presented in attractive terms. Historian Ira Berlin has affirmed that "emigration found an increasingly large following" among blacks "in the decade before the Civil War. . . . Reluctantly, some free Negroes looked for a new home where they might find a modicum of freedom, new opportunities, and a taste of manhood. '[I] cannot be a man heare and . . . I am ready to go if I live on bread and warter or die the never day i get there,' declared a Liberia-bound black."[8]

White antislavery leaders were often ambivalent. In 1828, William Lloyd Garrison suggested that federal funds should be appropriated for "the transportation of such liberated slaves and free colored people as are desirious of emigrating to a more congenial clime." But a few years afterward, he changed his mind: he attacked the American Colonization Society as "steeped in sin [and] deep in pollution."[9]

Proslavery Americans were also divided on the subject. Some believed it was a very wise measure to deport free blacks since their presence could exacerbate the restlessness of the enslaved: it could incite them to rebel or run away. But other slaveholders feared that the vision of a promised land in Liberia could have the very same effect or worse: a South Carolinian opined that any program of "bounties for Emancipation here, and transportation to Liberia afterwards" would constitute a "*peaceful* standard of servile revolt" in the slaveholding south.[10]

Lincoln endorsed the goal of colonization in the course of an 1852 eulogy for Henry Clay, the great congressional leader and presidential candidate who served for many years as the American Colonization Society's president. Lincoln cited scripture in his eulogy:

Pharaoh's country was cursed with plagues, and his hosts were drowned in the Red Sea for striving to retain a captive people who had already served them more than four hundred years. May like disasters never befall us! If as the friends of colonization hope, the present and coming generations of our country-men shall . . . succeed in freeing our land from the dangerous presence of slavery; and, at the same time, in restoring a captive people to their long-lost father-land, with bright prospects for the future; and this too, so gradually, that neither races nor individuals shall have suffered by the change, it will indeed be a glorious consummation.[11]

Some observers might regard such views as racist. Others might regard them as a combination of humanitarianism and prudence. Only further analysis and much more evidence can lead to responsible conclusions.

THE 1854 PEORIA SPEECH
AND ITS CONTEXT

A famous Lincoln speech that was largely devoted to blacks
contains a passage that is deeply ambiguous. The speech was
delivered on October 16, 1854, in Peoria, Illinois. It was a classic oration of the Free Soil movement—a strong antislavery speech.

But it was more: it was a passionate plea to white supremacists to
put aside racial bias when it came to freedom.

The speech was part of an enormous backlash against the Kansas-
Nebraska Act, a creation of Senator Stephen A. Douglas of Illinois. (It
bears noting that the act was amended under pressure from slave-state
leaders in Congress.) This act repealed the Missouri Compromise of
1820–21. It permitted slavery to spread into parts of the Louisiana
Purchase where the institution had been banned for over thirty
years. White settlers would have to decide for themselves if they
wished to own slaves. This particular policy or doctrine was known
as "popular sovereignty."

Both Democratic and Whig Free Soilers reviled this act. So Douglas made a statewide tour of Illinois to defend the legislation and to
mend political fences. He used a number of arguments to mollify
Free Soil opinion. He said it was unlikely that slavery would spread
to the prairies. But he also said he didn't care about the issue since
the fate of blacks was unimportant. Inferior races, said Douglas,
deserved almost anything they got. So whites, he continued, should
live and let live when it came to the ownership of blacks. White

majorities, he said, should decide this matter for themselves in every territory and state.

Lincoln followed Douglas and delivered sequential speeches attacking him. The speech that he gave in Peoria was published in the newspapers.

Lincoln went after Douglas right away on a fundamental issue: the issue of blacks' humanity. "The Judge," he said—referring to Douglas's earlier service on the Illinois Supreme Court—"has no very vivid impression that the negro is a human. . . . In his view, the question of whether a new country shall be slave or free, is a matter of as utter indifference, as it is whether his neighbor shall plant his farm with tobacco, or stock it with horned cattle."[1]

Lincoln used the same device in alluding to the leaders of the slave states; "equal justice to the South," he said, "requires us to consent to the extending of slavery to new countries. That is to say, inasmuch as you do not object to my taking my hog to Nebraska, therefore I must not object to you taking your slave. Now, I admit this is perfectly logical, if there is no difference between hogs and negroes. But while you thus require me to deny the humanity of the negro, I wish to ask whether you of the south yourselves, have ever been willing to do as much?"[2]

Lincoln probed the southern conscience by asking why slaves were ever freed by certain guilt-ridden masters in the South. "There are in the United States and territories," Lincoln pointed out, "433,643 free blacks. . . . How comes this vast amount of property to be running around without owners? We do not see free horses or free cattle running at large. How is this? All these free blacks are the descendants of slaves, or have been slaves themselves, and they would be slaves now, except for SOMETHING which has operated on their white owners, inducing them, at vast pecuniary sacrifices, to liberate them" (original emphasis).[3]

He continued with greater intensity: "What is that SOMETHING? Is there any mistaking it? In all these cases it is your sense of justice, and human sympathy, continually telling you, that the poor negro has some natural right to himself—that those who deny it, and make mere merchandise of him, deserve kickings, contempt and death."

"If the negro is a *man*," Lincoln told his listeners, "my ancient faith teaches me that 'all men are created equal'" (original emphasis).[4]

Lincoln's insistence that "the negro is a *man*"—his insistence that blacks were not livestock or "merchandise"—must be understood as a significant attack upon "scientific racism," a powerful and rising international movement with proto-Nazi affinities. It was a white-supremacist movement that regarded certain races as "subhuman."

Dr. Samuel G. Morton, an American participant, assembled a collection of human skulls in the 1840s for the purpose of comparing the cranial capacities of whites and their racial "inferiors." Morton influenced the famous Louis Agassiz, a Swiss-born scientist who became an American rival of Charles Darwin.[5] Agassiz indeed became a major proponent of "polygenism," the theory that the races of the human family are separate biological species. Another "polygenist" was Dr. Josiah Nott, a physician who propounded his theories in articles for southern journals such as *De Bow's Review*. Nott also coauthored a polygenist book—*Types of Mankind*—that appeared in the very same year as the Kansas-Nebraska Act, the year when Lincoln lashed out at Douglas.[6]

One prominent member of the polygenist movement claimed that he had influenced Douglas. In 1853, Dr. John H. Van Evrie, a New York physician, wrote a pamphlet entitled *Negroes and Negro "Slavery": The First, an Inferior Race; the Latter Its Normal Condition*. The 1861 edition begins as follows: "To the White Men of America,—There are now thirty millions of white men, twelve millions of negroes, and perhaps twelve millions of Indians or Aborigines, in America. God has made these white men, Indians, and negroes, just what we see they are—just what our senses, as well as our instincts and our reason show us they are—different creatures, different *species*" (original emphasis).[7]

In 1863, Van Evrie claimed that "the late Senator Douglas [had] distributed a considerable number of copies" of this pamphlet.[8]

The Peoria speech made Lincoln's opinion of such pseudoscientific racists—people who claimed that the "normal condition" of blacks was enslavement—clear in the extreme; in Lincoln's estimation, all those who made "merchandise" of blacks deserved "kickings, contempt and death" because the negro "is a *man*."

Lincoln tried to invoke patriotic sentiments to counteract racist opinion. "Nearly eighty years ago," he lectured the crowd in Peoria, "we began by declaring that all men are created equal; but now . . . we have run down to the other declaration that for SOME to enslave OTHERS is a 'sacred right of self-government.'" But the conscience of humanity must find such a doctrine repulsive, Lincoln insisted. "It will still be the abundance of man's heart," he intoned, "that slavery extension is wrong; and out of the abundance of his heart, his mouth will continue to speak."[9]

This was powerful rhetoric—a fighting speech—but then Lincoln began to change the subject: he turned from slavery *extension* in the western lands to the existing institution in the South. And the words that he spoke have given critics down the years the impression that his deep humanitarianism was tempered by bigotry. Here is what he said:

> If all earthly power were given me, I should not know what to do, as to the existing institution. My first impulse would be to free all the slaves, and send them to Liberia,—to their own native land. But a moment's reflection would convince me, that whatever of high hope, (as I think there is) there may be in this, in the long run, its sudden execution is impossible. If they were all landed there in a day, they would all perish in the next ten days; and there are not surplus shipping and surplus money enough in the world to carry them there in many times ten days. What then? Free them all, and keep them among us as underlings? Is it quite certain that this betters their condition? I think I would not hold one in slavery, at any rate; yet the point is not clear enough for me to denounce people upon. What next? Free them, and make them politically and socially, our equals? My own feelings will not admit of this; and if mine would, we well know that those of the great mass of white people will not. Whether this feeling accords with justice and sound judgment, is not the sole question, if indeed, it is any part of it. A universal feeling, whether well or ill-founded, can not be safely disregarded.[10]

Lincoln said that his "feelings" would "not admit" the idea that blacks should share the political and social status of whites. This sentence by itself sounds racist.

Yet, the sentence in question *cannot* be read by itself, for it was part of a much-longer passage—as we have just seen.

As political philosopher Harry V. Jaffa once observed, when Lincoln said that his feelings would "not admit" the scenario of social and political equality for blacks, "he immediately introduced, as a hypothetical possibility, that his own feelings might not be against it. Why? The sentence, taken as a whole, is an equivocation."[11]

When Lincoln referred to his "feelings," he did not describe them. But he never said his feelings amounted to revulsion toward blacks as such.

Instead, he stated that *when and if* his feelings might support the proposition of black civil rights, the white-supremacy culture would oppose him. Then he raised the question—in a seemingly noncommittal way—as to whether racial bias was grounded in the principles of "justice and sound judgment."

This passage, on its merits, raises serious questions of intent. Why, after all, would a racist choose to speak in this manner and especially so in antebellum Illinois? Lincoln seemed to be saying that the "feeling" of whites in regard to racial issues might be ill-grounded—unjust.

Why take such a risk if Lincoln shared the common "feeling"? There were other ways to challenge Stephen Douglas. Lincoln could have used the much easier theme that kept resounding through the Free Soil movement: the threat of slavery to working-class whites. He could have savaged Douglas for lowering the floodgates that held back the tide of black migration. Instead, he spoke of "sympathy" for every "poor negro" who deserved the "right to himself."

Why would a racist choose to do such a thing in Illinois?

Two opposite theories could account for the behavior of Lincoln. Theory number 1: Lincoln was at odds with himself—he was struggling to overcome bigotry. One historian has suggested that the struggle of Lincoln with a "self-admitted racism" was honest—even gallant. It was a struggle with "something of the transcending dignity of Huck Finn's." Lincoln, in this view, would not allow his prejudice to "cloud his sense of blacks' full humanity."[12]

Theory number 2: Lincoln was engaging in a justified deception; he was testing the limits of prejudice. He was trying to establish safe political ground from which to challenge his listeners, to goad them into questioning the nature of the "feeling," and to ask themselves if it was just.

These rival theories are tested in the course of the chapters to follow. But one final piece of evidence from 1854 must be presented.

Circa 1854—the attribution of the piece to this year represented an educated guess by the editors of Lincoln's *Collected Works*—Lincoln penned a meditation on race as related to slavery.

> If A. can prove, however conclusively, that he may, of right, enslave B., why may not B. snatch the same argument, and prove equally, that he may enslave A.?—You say A. is white, and B. is black. It is *color*, then; the lighter, having the right to enslave the darker? Take care. By this rule, you are to be the slave of the first man you meet, with a fairer skin than your own. You do not mean *color* exactly—You mean that whites are *intellectually* the superior of blacks, and, therefore, have the right to enslave them? Take care again. By this rule, you are to be slave to the first man you meet, with an intellect superior to your own.[13]

Lincoln seemed to be saying that a broad range of differentiae—gradations ranging from pigmentation to intellect—neutralized the boundaries of race. *Individual* differences, he seemed to be saying, were the ones that possessed the most importance. Hence, the *man* who possesses a fairer skin and the *man* who outclasses one in intellect will trump the racial ideologists. These, Lincoln seemed to be saying—these encounters of unique individuals—are antecedent to all racial patterns. And especially so in a republic that proclaimed a self-evident truth: men are equal in their right to seek happiness but never at the cost of reducing one another to the status of beasts of the field.

CHAPTER THREE

THE 1857 SPRINGFIELD
SPEECH AND ITS CONTEXT

O f all the Lincoln speeches on slavery and race, one speech is the most contradictory: a speech that was delivered at the invitation of some fellow Republicans—for Lincoln by then had joined the new Republican Party—in the Illinois capital of Springfield on June 26, 1857.

The Republican Party had been founded in reaction to the Kansas-Nebraska Act. It was a fusion party designed to unite the Free Soilers from each of the existing parties: the Democrats and the Whigs. The Whig Party disintegrated after the Republican Party was founded, though the Democrats survived.

In 1856, the new Republican Party was strong enough to run a presidential candidate. But then the party was jolted by a soon-to-be-infamous Supreme Court decision: the 1857 *Dred Scott* decision, which held that both Congress and the territorial legislatures were powerless to stop the spread of slavery. This decision was also a threat to the politics of Democrats like Stephen Douglas, whose doctrine of popular sovereignty rested on the premise that the territorial settlers could decide about slavery for themselves.

But in one respect the *Dred Scott* decision was consistent with the politics of Douglas: it was a virulently racist decision. Chief Justice Roger B. Taney asserted that blacks had no constitutional rights that the white man was bound to respect.

As he struggled to reconcile popular sovereignty with *Dred Scott* principles, Douglas fell back upon the demagoguery of race. He kept asserting that the Republicans—"Black Republicans," he called them—were "negro lovers," whose opposition to the spread of slavery would lead to "race mixing." He said that people like Lincoln had a stealthy plan to force emancipation, to be followed by the "amalgamation" of blacks into white society. Black voting rights and racial intermarriage would follow as a matter of course. This was an inflammatory message to send to the Illinois electorate.

Lincoln was recruited to respond to such charges and attack the *Dred Scott* decision; this was the occasion of the speech that he gave in Springfield, Illinois, on June 26, 1857.

For those who study the conundrum of Lincoln and race, this speech is a troubling document. Far more than the Peoria speech, it forces us to wonder what Lincoln's inner feelings toward blacks and other races might have been.

On the positive side, Lincoln vilified the *Dred Scott* decision for its gross inhumanity and urged his audience to empathize with the enslaved. He used a metaphor—the slave was like a man who had been locked up in prison for life:

> They have him in his prison house; they have searched his person, and left no prying instrument with him. One after another they have closed the heavy iron doors upon him, and now they have him, as it were, bolted in with a lock of a hundred keys, which can never be unlocked without the concurrence of every key; the keys are in the hands of a hundred different men, and they [have] scattered in a hundred different and distant places; and they stand musing as to what invention, in all the dominions of mind and matter, can be produced to make the impossibility of his escape more complete than it is.[1]

Then Lincoln zeroed in on Douglas for asserting that the Declaration of Independence—its equality clause, in particular—was intended to apply to whites only.

Since Lincoln had used the nation's founding document to spread the idea that there was something un-American in slavery, Douglas asserted that the Declaration was rhetorical shorthand contrived for the purpose of separating from the British Empire and for no other purpose whatsoever; the proclamation that all men are created equal, said Douglas, meant that whites in America were equal to the whites in the British Isles.

Rubbish, said Lincoln; the Declaration's rhetoric was world-redemptive in intention. Attacking both Taney and Douglas, Lincoln strove to rebut them as follows: "Chief Justice Taney admits that the language of the Declaration is broad enough to include the whole human family, but he and Judge Douglas argue that the authors of that instrument did not intend to include negroes, by the fact that they did not, at once, actually place them on an equality with the whites. Now this grave argument comes to just nothing at all, by the other fact, that they did not at once, *or ever afterwards*, actually place all white people on an equality with one another" (original emphasis).[2]

Lincoln reasoned that the signers of the Declaration meant "to include *all* men, but they did not intend to declare all men equal *in all respects*. They did not mean to say all were equal in color, size, intellect, moral developments, or social capacity. They defined with tolerable distinctness, in what respects they did consider all men created equal—equal in 'certain unalienable rights among which are life, liberty, and the pursuit of happiness.' This they said, and this they meant" (original emphasis).[3] Lincoln went on to deliver an oracular statement of ideals. The founders, he said, never tried to assert "the obvious untruth, that all men were then actually enjoying that equality, nor yet, that they were about to confer it immediately upon them. In fact they had no power to confer such a boon." But they meant to "declare the *right*, so that the *enforcement* of it might follow as fast as circumstances should permit. They meant to set up a standard maxim for free society, which should be familiar to all, and revered by all; constantly looked to, constantly labored for, and even though never perfectly attained, constantly approximated, and thereby constantly spreading and deepening its influence, and augmenting the happiness and value of life to all people of all colors everywhere" (original emphasis).[4]

Lincoln's intuition was correct in regard to this matter, for Thomas Jefferson—the author of the Declaration of Independence—wrote privately that the Declaration's equality credo must be incrementally applied. "The ground of liberty is to be gained by inches," Jefferson wrote: "We must be contented to secure what we can get from time to time, and eternally press forward for what is yet to get."[5] So much for the positive thrust of this important Lincoln speech. But the Springfield speech contained some other statements that appear to be confessions of bigotry.

Lincoln was never "race-baiting" as he uttered these statements. He was on the defensive: fending off the demagoguery of Douglas, who was stoking the fires of white-supremacist hatred.

Lincoln was responding to the "race-mixing" charge: the charge that the Republicans were pushing American whites down the slippery slope that would lead to intermarriage with blacks (it bears noting that Illinois had passed a law that made racial intermarriage illegal). Douglas, said Lincoln, was pandering to the "natural disgust in the minds of nearly all white people, to the idea of an indiscriminate amalgamation of the races." He was "evidently . . . basing his chief hope, upon the chances of being able to appropriate the benefits of this disgust." Well, said Lincoln, this tactic wouldn't work, for its premises were illogical:

> If he [Douglas] can, by much drumming and repeating, fasten the odium of that idea upon his adversaries, he thinks he can struggle through the storm. He therefore clings to this hope, as a drowning man to the last plank. . . . He finds the Republicans insisting that the Declaration of Independence includes ALL men, black as well as white; and forthwith he boldly denies that it includes negroes at all, and proceeds to argue gravely that all who contend it does, do so only because they want to vote, and eat, and sleep, and marry with negroes! . . . Now I protest against the counterfeit logic which concludes that, because I do not want a black woman for a *slave* I must necessarily want her for a *wife*. I need not have her for either, I can just leave her alone. In some respects she certainly is not my equal; but in her natural right to eat the bread she earns with her own hands without asking leave of anyone else, she is my equal, and the equal of all others. (original emphasis)[6]

She is "not my equal" in "some respects," Lincoln said. Here is a statement that could certainly seem to be racist.

And here is another, a statement that is even more provocative. "Judge Douglas," said Lincoln, "is especially horrified at the thought of the mixing of the blood by the white and black races: agreed for once—a thousand times agreed."[7]

Well: it would seem as if Lincoln shared the visceral aversion toward blacks—in this case a sexual aversion—that was typical in white Illinois. So if the "Huck Finn" theory of Lincoln's racial attitudes is true—the theory that Lincoln was struggling to overcome revulsion toward people of other races—here is evidence.

But what about the opposite theory: that Lincoln was *pretending* to feelings such as these to keep the force of prejudice contained—to contain it enough to make his white-supremacist listeners focus on the monstrous injustice of enslaving other people?

One fact that could support such a view is Lincoln's introduction of humor. The very same Lincoln who declared that he was "horrified" by the prospect of racial intermarriage made jokes about the subject in the course of the Springfield speech. So how "horrified" could he have been?

To be sure, racists often use humor—vicious humor, as everybody knows—but the humor that Lincoln employed was benign. Lincoln said that there were "fortunately white men enough to marry all the white women, and black men enough to marry all the black women, so let them be married. . . . On this point we fully agree with the judge."[8]

Is this the talk of a man who was phobic about "race-mixing"? Would a man who was "horrified" by racial intermarriage make light of it with whimsical humor? Perhaps—the human mind can be eccentric. But this matter would appear to be ambiguous.

So, too, is the clear-sounding statement in regard to the hypothetical black woman who was "not my equal" in "some respects." If Lincoln meant what the audience probably (nay, undoubtedly) heard as they listened to him speak—that blacks were less endowed with intelligence than whites—he was certainly in line with the thinking of the following Republicans:

- U.S. Representative Owen Lovejoy of Illinois: "I know very well that the African race, as a race, is not equal to ours . . . [not equal] in gracefulness of motion, or loveliness of feature; not in mental endowment, moral susceptibility, and emotional power."[9]
- U.S. Senator Henry Wilson of Massachusetts: "I do not believe in the equality of the African with the white race, mentally or physically, and I do not think morally."[10]
- U.S. Senator William H. Seward of New York: "The great fact is now fully realized that the African race here is a foreign and feeble element like the Indians, incapable of assimilation."[11]

Lincoln's statement ("she certainly is not my equal") would appear to fit this climate of opinion.

But if, for the sake of the argument—and this is a matter for a nuanced and reasoned conjecture—Lincoln was trying to deceive his racist listeners by saying things that they insisted on hearing, his statement might be less than it appeared. If he was consciously "faking it" to rob Douglas of his race-mongering advantage—if Lincoln was making concessions to popular prejudice without any genuine enthusiasm or agreement—then his statement was in fact very slippery.

When Lincoln declared that the black woman was "not my equal" in "some respects," he never tried to define these "respects," and he never even defined the crucial term *equal.*

This is not just a matter of semantics. The term *equal* can be used in three senses—senses that can overlap or diverge. It depends on the actual intent of the person who puts the term to use. First, *equal* can denote an identity in abstract relations, as when Thomas Jefferson declared that all men are created equal in regard to their natural rights. Second, *equal* can connote an identity of innate attributes. Lincoln used the term in this way when he denied that men were "equal in color, size"—another Lincoln joke, surely, for Lincoln's great height stood in humorous contrast to Douglas's diminutive stature—"intellect, moral developments, or social capacity." Third, *equal* can denote an identity of status, as when Lincoln observed that the founders lacked the power to *place* all men "on an equality."

Which sense of this ambiguous term was Lincoln using when he said the hypothetical black woman was not his equal in some respects? Did he mean that she lacked the same abilities that he possessed? Or can his statement be interpreted differently? It could if Lincoln felt himself forced to parrot ugly formulations under pressure from an odious opponent. In such an event, he might concoct very slippery language that contained alternative meanings.

If Lincoln shared the overall prejudice of whites in Illinois, then the statement about the black woman is clear. But if Lincoln did not share the prejudice, the best that he could do in these circumstances—if he meant to wield power—was to say what his listeners expected to hear but to say it with minimal, innocuous language that possesses what we would call "deniability."

His language was minimal indeed if compared to the words of Lovejoy. That Republican congressman spelled it out clearly when he said that blacks in his opinion were unequal to whites in the "gracefulness of motion . . . loveliness of feature . . . mental endowment, moral susceptibility, and emotional power." Lincoln never made statements like that. To the contrary: his statements on racial "inequality" were open-ended and vague, perhaps deliberately vague.

Perhaps the statement on the black woman's "inequality" is truly the statement of a racist. Or perhaps it is the statement of a clever and adroit politician who could claim, if he wished, that he only meant to say that black women had been thrust far lower in the sociopolitical hierarchy of the times: they were not his "equals" in *status*—which was just a simple statement of fact.

Was Lincoln such a tricky politician? Douglas believed that he was. In the following year—1858—Douglas declared that Lincoln was a secret "negro lover" and a master of evasion on the subject—a man, to cite Douglas's backhanded compliment, possessing a "fertile genius in devising language to conceal his thoughts."[12]

Was this true? One cannot really tell from the Springfield speech, and so the next block of evidence must come from the Lincoln-Douglas debates, which took place in the following year. These debates permit the examination of Douglas's complaint in its immediate context: the issue of race as it figures in their great oratorical battle.

THE LINCOLN-DOUGLAS DEBATES

Abraham Lincoln hoped to throw Stephen Douglas out of the U.S. Senate. Lincoln felt that Douglas deserved to be punished for his role in destroying the Missouri Compromise. So in the summer of 1858, Lincoln challenged Douglas to a series of debates that would be held between August and October in different parts of Illinois. The central issue was slavery. And the corollary issues were Free Soil, popular sovereignty, the Kansas-Nebraska Act, the *Dred Scott* decision, and—above all—race.

On July 10, Lincoln gave a kick-off address in Chicago at a torch-light rally—a speech that he delivered from a window balcony of Tremont House hotel. It was a Free Soil classic. The passages with racial significance deserve to be quoted at length.

Audience reactions were recorded by journalists using shorthand. And they used the same method later on in the Lincoln-Douglas debates. Here is Lincoln in action on July 10, speaking to a large degree extemporaneously:

> Now, sirs, for the purpose of squaring things with this idea of "don't care if slavery is voted up or down," for sustaining the Dred Scott decision (A voice—"Hit him again"), for holding that the Declaration of Independence did not mean anything at all, we have Judge Douglas giving his exposition of what the Declaration of Independence means, and we have him saying that the people of America are equal to the people of England. According to his construction, you Germans are not connected with it.

This was clever; Lincoln drove a conceptual wedge—the wedge of ethnicity—into white-supremacist ranks. And having broken up the pattern of white solidarity, he reassembled things:

> Now I ask in all soberness, if all these things, if indulged in, if ratified, if confirmed and endorsed, if taught to our children, and repeated to them, do not tend to rub out the sentiment of liberty in this country, and to transform this Government into a government of some other form. Those arguments that are made, that the inferior race are to be treated with as much allowance as they are capable of enjoying; that as much is to be done for them as their condition will allow. What are these arguments? They are the arguments that kings have made for enslaving the people in all ages of the world. You will find that all the arguments in favor of king-craft were of this class; they always bestrode the necks of the people, not that they wanted to do it, but because the people were better off for being ridden.

Lincoln added ethics and religion to the patriotic theme he had established; slavery, he said, was like the serpent in Eden, and it threatened the principle that underlay America's equality creed; it was a threat to the golden rule itself:

> That is their argument, and this argument of the Judge is the same old serpent that says you work and I eat, you toil and I will enjoy the fruits of it. Turn it whatever way you will—whether it come from the mouth of a King, an excuse for enslaving the people of his country, or from the mouth of men of one race as a reason for enslaving the men of another race, it is all the same old serpent, and I hold if that course of argumentation that is made for the purpose of convincing the public mind that we should not care about this, should be granted, it does not stop with the negro. I should like to know if taking this old Declaration of Independence, which declares that all men are equal upon principle and making exceptions to it where will it stop. If one man says it does not mean a negro, why not another say it does not mean some other man? If that declaration is

not the truth, let us get the Statute book, in which we find it and tear it out! Who is so bold as to do it! (Voices—"me" "no one," &c.) If it is not true let us tear it out! (cries of "no, no,").

Lincoln ended with a plea to discard racial thinking entirely: "Let us discard all this quibbling about this man and the other man—this race and that race and the other race being inferior, and therefore they must be placed in an inferior position. . . . Let us discard all these things, and unite as one people throughout this land, until we shall once more stand up declaring that all men are created equal."[1]

Lincoln's emphasis on human—not racial—solidarity contrasted with the racist ferocity of Douglas. Just the day before Lincoln's Chicago address, Douglas called the United States a nation of "white people—people composed of European descendants—a people that have established this government for themselves and their posterity, and I am in favor of preserving not only the purity of the blood, but the purity of the government from any admixture or amalgamation with inferior races."[2]

A week after Lincoln's Chicago address, Douglas spoke at greater length about "inferior races" in a speech that he delivered in Springfield. Asians and Native Americans, he said, deserved the very same exclusion from "government" that people with an African background deserved: "I am opposed to Indian equality. I am opposed to putting the coolies, now importing into this country, on an equality with us, or putting the Chinese or any other inferior race on an equality with us."[3]

At a stop in Bloomington, with Lincoln in attendance, Douglas whipped up the crowd with the ultimate horror of horrors—racial intermarriage—and he attacked Lincoln's joke about the fact that there were white men enough to marry all the white women and black men enough to marry all the black women: "He would permit them to marry, would he not? And if he gives them that right, I suppose he will let them marry whom they please, provided they marry their equals. If the divine law declares that the white man is the equal of the negro woman, that they are on a perfect equality, I suppose he admits the right of the negro woman to marry the white man."[4] And then black men could marry . . . white women.

When he arrived in Springfield, Douglas kept working the issue; he warned that Republicans like Lincoln might attempt to repeal the law banning racial intermarriage. If so, then the state of Illinois would be lost. "When he lets down the bars," said Douglas, then the "floods shall have turned in upon us and covered our prairies thick with them till they [the prairies] shall be as dark and black as night in mid-day. . . . We must preserve the purity of the race not only in our politics but in our domestic relations."[5]

Lincoln evidently sensed—perhaps from the audience reactions—that he had to go onto the defensive. So after Douglas's speech, he replied with what appears to be a carefully composed disclaimer. "Last night," Lincoln said, presumably alluding to Douglas's Bloomington address, "Judge Douglas tormented himself with horrors about my disposition to make negroes perfectly equal with white men in social and political relations. He did not stop to show that I have said any such thing, or that it legitimately follows from anything I have said, but he rushes in with his assertions. I adhere to the Declaration of Independence. If Judge Douglas and his friends are not willing to stand by it, let them come up and amend it. Let them make it read that all men are created equal except negroes."

Lincoln continued with a statement that deserves extended analysis: "Certainly the negro is not our equal in color—perhaps not in other respects; still, in the right to put into his mouth the bread that his own hands have earned, he is the equal of every other man, white or black. . . . All I ask for the negro is that if you do not like him, let him alone."[6]

If Lincoln were an unabashed racist, this statement was tepid, so tepid that it justifies a conditional hypothesis that Lincoln was *not* an unabashed racist. But if the Huck Finn theory is correct—the theory that Lincoln was a tortured and conflicted soul, half bigot and half humanitarian—then his speech contained precisely the "quibbling" in regard to "this man and the other man—this race and that race and the other race being inferior"—that Lincoln himself had disavowed in his Chicago speech.

The alternative theory—perhaps we should call it the "master politician" theory—should also be considered if we wish to make sense of Lincoln's statement. For if Lincoln didn't feel any racial bias but knew that he had to say *something* to calm his touchy audience or else be jeered off the stage (and out of politics), then his statement in the Springfield speech was an adroit maneuver of evasion, for it conveyed alternative meanings. It was possibly the language of a clever attorney who had learned, in the course of drafting contracts for clients who required some slippery text, how to extricate himself from tight places through an artful use of words: through pettifoggery.

So let us analyze the following formulation as to meaning: "Certainly the negro is not our equal in color—perhaps not in other respects." The word *certainly* is clear, but what else concerning blacks was really "certain" in Lincoln's estimation? That the Negro is "not our equal in color." But again, the word *equal* was ambiguous. Moreover, since personal taste in color is subjective, this phrase could be related to the plea that Lincoln made at the end of his statement: "All I ask for the negro is that if you do not like him, let him alone." This statement could mean that one should make oneself ignore those things about the Negro that are not to one's taste, like his color.

In any case, the upshot appears to be this: if "inequality" in *color* was "certain," *no other differences* between the two races in Lincoln's estimation were "certain." For after Lincoln's introductory clause ("certainly the negro is not our equal in color"), he dismissed the whole subject with the following shrug of the shoulders, as it were: "perhaps not in other respects."

Note the fudge word—the weasel word—*perhaps*. Lincoln seemed to be saying that he didn't really know if there were differences in race beyond color. Lincoln's qualifier term—*perhaps*—would be heard by many in the sense that perhaps such differences do exist but with the flip-side corollary left to be inferred by discerning minds. Perhaps they do not.

Lincoln wrote a very interesting private reflection that suggests that he was searching his soul in regard to the racist hypothesis, not least of all the hypothesis as advanced by eminent scientists like Louis Agassiz. This statement in some respects—but not in others—might appear to substantiate the Huck Finn theory of Lincoln the tortured soul. "Suppose it is true," Lincoln wrote at some point during 1858, "that the negro is inferior to the white, in the gifts of nature; is it not the exact reverse [of] justice that the white should, for that reason, take from the negro, any part of the little which has been given him?"[7]

In addition to noticing the word *suppose*—equivalent here to the use of *perhaps* in the speech that was just examined—there are two ways to take this reflection. Either Lincoln was responding to a prompting of the heart (or the gut), an inner *sense* that kept telling him that blacks were inferior, or else he was responding to the language that he heard all around him in Illinois and elsewhere—not only from demagogues like Douglas but from fellow Republicans like William Seward and Owen Lovejoy, who took it for granted that blacks, as a race, were inferior. What is notable here is the reflective candor prompting Lincoln to tell himself "suppose." *He did not really know* whether differences in anything but color really separated races.

What he did know, however—it was surely a prompting of the heart, for he never said otherwise—was this: blacks are human beings, and they deserve the basic decency of treatment that every single one of us deserves. Surely, Lincoln was attempting to elicit that prompting from the heart of every person in an audience he spoke to, that prompting of the conscience that arises in us all, except in people whose sense is blocked by psychopathology, or ideology, or overweening malice, or other impediments, the sense that we should treat one another with decency and grace, as Saul Bellow's character Artur Sammler would put it a century later when he spoke of the "contract" whose terms we all know in our "inmost heart . . . for that is the truth of it—that we all know, God, that we know, that we know, we know, we know."[8]

In August, the series of formal debates between Lincoln and Douglas began. And Douglas was in quintessential form as he worked the enormous crowd on August 21 in the Illinois town of Ottawa:

> I ask you, are you in favor of conferring upon the negro the rights and privileges of citizenship? ("No, no.") Do you desire to strike out of our State Constitution the clause which keeps slaves and free negroes out of the State, and allow the free negroes to flow in, ("never") and cover your prairies with black

settlements? Do you desire to turn this beautiful State into a free negro colony, ("no, no") in order that when Missouri abolishes slavery she can send one hundred thousand emancipated slaves into Illinois, to become citizens and voters, on an equality with yourselves? ("Never," "no.") If you desire negro citizenship . . . then support Mr. Lincoln and the Black Republican party. . . . For one, I am opposed to negro citizenship in any and every form. (Cheers.) I believe this government was made on the white basis. ("Good.") I believe it was made by white men, for the benefit of white men and their posterity forever.[9]

Douglas also referred to Mr. Lincoln's "conscientious belief that the negro was made his equal, and hence is his brother, (laughter) but for my own part, I do not regard the negro as my equal, and positively deny that he is my brother or any kin to me whatever. ('Never.' 'Hit him again,' and cheers)."[10]

Is this dose of Mr. Douglas's rhetoric enough to catch the force of his charismatic bigotry? No, it isn't. Here is Douglas on the subject of interracial sex in his next debate with Lincoln, on August 27, in the town of Freeport, Illinois. This was mostly a Republican town, which Douglas knew. But it was part of his strategy to dish out bigotry all over the state, so he could brag about saying the same thing everywhere, compared to Lincoln's shifty evasions:

The last time I came here to make a speech, while talking from the stand to you, people of Freeport, as I am doing to-day, I saw a carriage and a magnificent one it was, drive up and take a position outside the crowd; a beautiful young lady was sitting on the box seat, whilst Fred. Douglass [he was referring to the black abolitionist Frederick Douglass] and her mother reclined inside, and the owner of the carriage acted as driver. (Laughter, cheers, cries of right, what have you to say against it, &c.) I saw this in your own town. ("What of it.") All I have to say is this, that if you, Black Republicans, think that the negro ought to be on a social equality with your wives and daughters, and ride in a carriage with your wife, whilst you drive the team, you have a perfect right to do so.[11]

The salacious allusion to interracial sex was unmistakable. It is interesting to note that just a year before the Lincoln-Douglas debates, *Madame Bovary* by Gustave Flaubert rolled off the press in 1857. One of the unforgettable scenes in this novel is the scene in which the title character is ravished in a carriage by one of her adulterous lovers. Perhaps Douglas had read—or heard about—the book.

Douglas used the very same story down in southern Illinois, where racial animosities were deeper; many whites in the area had come from the nearby slave states of Tennessee and Kentucky. And they brought their racial attitudes with them. Here is Douglas on September 15 in the town of Jonesboro:

> In the extreme northern counties they brought out men to canvass the State whose complexion suited their political creed, and hence Fred Douglass, the negro, was to be found there. . . . Why, they brought Fred Douglass to Freeport when I was addressing a meeting there in a carriage driven by a white owner, the negro sitting inside with the white lady and her daughter. ("Shame") When I got through canvassing the northern counties that year [1854] and progressed as far south as Springfield, I was met and opposed in discussion by Lincoln, Lovejoy, Trumbull, and Sidney Breese, who were on the one side (Laughter.) Father Giddings, the high priest of abolitionism, had just been there, and Chase came about the time I left. ("Why didn't you shoot him?") I did take a running shot at them, but as I was single-handed against the white, black and mixed drove, I had to use a short gun and fire into the crowd instead of taking them off singly with a rifle. (Great laughter and cheers).

Then Douglas recited his litany of breeds who deserved to be regarded as "inferior"; he said the signers of the Declaration of Independence "had no reference either to the negro, the savage Indians, the Fejee, the Malay, or any other inferior and degraded race."[12]

How did Lincoln answer this abuse? In two ways: he made light of it with humor whenever he could, and he disavowed plans or intentions to promote civil rights legislation.

Here is an example of his humor: at Charleston, Illinois, on September 16, Lincoln said he did not know of "any place where an alteration of the social and political relations of the negro and the white man can be made except in the State Legislature." And since "Judge Douglas seems to be in constant horror that some such danger is rapidly approaching, I propose as the best means to prevent it that the Judge be kept at home and placed in the State legislature to fight the measure. (Uproarious laughter and applause.) I do not propose dwelling any longer at this time on the subject."[13]

And now the famous or infamous Lincoln disavowal—a statement that Lincoln used repeatedly to make the ugly issue of race go away ("I do not propose dwelling any longer at this time on the subject") so he could focus on the evil of slavery: "I have no purpose to introduce political and social equality between the white and the black races. There is a physical difference between the two, which in my judgment will probably forever forbid their living together upon the footing of a perfect equality, and inasmuch as it becomes a necessity that there must be a difference, I, as well as Judge Douglas, am in favor of the race to which I belong, having the superior position."[14]

Of all the Lincoln statements that appear to be racist, this is probably the one that is cited most often, by racists (like U.S. Senator James K. Vardaman) and by antiracists (like journalist Lerone Bennett Jr.). Out of context, it looks very bad. But within the full context—the context of all the many documents presented already—it would seem to fit the master-politician theory well. For this recital was a passionless statement—formalistic, if not formulaic. And it is full of exceptionally slippery, ambiguous, and legalistic language that could well be the language of evasion.

Just how would it have worked, this evasion? If Lincoln was indeed playing games with his audience, the gambit could have worked like this. Sentence 1: "I have no purpose to introduce political and social equality between the white and the black races." Translation: I have no intention at the moment of espousing civil rights, since the effort would be doomed to failure and the cost would be political suicide. Sentence 2, clause 1: "There is a physical difference between the two, which in my judgment will probably forever forbid their living together upon the footing of a perfect equality. . . ." Translation: The difference in color between the two races causes hatred so intense that racial harmony is probably impossible. Sentence 2, clause 2: ". . . and inasmuch as it becomes a necessity that there must be a difference, I, as well as Judge Douglas, am in favor of the race to which I belong, having the superior position." Translation: If the racial animosity devolves into a power struggle, only martyrs would choose subjugation.

Two years later, in Connecticut, however, Lincoln said that this particular premise—the premise that there "*must* be a difference" in the power positions of the races—was absurd. On March 5, 1860, he said that "the proposition that there is a struggle between the white man and the negro contains a falsehood. There *is* no struggle. *If* there was, I should be for the white man. If two men are adrift at sea on a plank which will bear up but one, the law justifies either in pushing the other off. I never had to struggle to keep a negro from enslaving me, nor did a negro have to fight to keep me from enslaving him."[15]

Two very different theories have now been presented—the Huck Finn theory and the master-politician theory—to account for Lincoln's statements on race. Perhaps a choice between the two cannot be made.

But on the other hand—perhaps it can.

THE 1859 COLUMBUS SPEECH

Though Douglas remained in the U.S. Senate—senators were chosen by the legislatures of the states, and the Democrats retained their control of the Illinois legislature in 1858—Lincoln's campaign began to make him a rising star in the Republican Party, a leader with a chance to get the 1860 presidential nomination. And in 1859, Lincoln started to consider the prospect.

To increase his chances, he made a series of speeches in lower-northern swing states, for such states held the key to electoral-college victory in 1860. And his speech in Columbus, Ohio, on September 16, 1859—a speech that deserves to be much better known—is one of the most important documents pertaining to Lincoln and race.

The key to this dimension of the Lincoln speech was yet another speech: a speech that was made by Stephen Douglas in the previous year. Douglas had his own presidential ambitions. And he was working very hard to increase his support base in the South. He needed to cultivate Southern support to have a chance at the 1860 Democratic nomination. Here is what Douglas said on November 30, 1858, in Memphis, Tennessee:

> If old Joshua Giddings [a prominent antislavery leader] should raise a colony in Ohio and settle down in Louisiana, he would be the strongest advocate of slavery in the whole South; he would find when he got there his opinion would be very much modified; he would find on those sugar plantations it was not

a question between the white man and the negro, but between the negro and the crocodile. He would say that between the negro and the crocodile, he took the side of the negro. But, between the negro and the white man, he would go for the white man.[1]

Lincoln brooded upon this statement and jotted down notes as he prepared for his Columbus speech. Here is Lincoln's first draft:

At Memphis, Douglas told his audience that he was for the negro against the crocodile, but for the white man against the negro. This was not a sudden thought spontaneously thrown off at Memphis. He said the same thing many times in Illinois last summer and autumn, though I am not sure it was reported then. It is a carefully framed illustration of the estimate he places on the negro and the manner in which he would have him dealt with. It is a sort of proposition in proportion. "*As* the negro is to the crocodile, *so* the white man is to the negro. As the negro ought to treat the crocodile as a beast, so the white man ought to treat the negro as a beast." (original emphasis)[2]

Lincoln used this material in his Columbus speech, and he raged against Douglas, whose doctrines, he said, were a threat to human liberty everywhere. Lincoln accused Douglas of softening and weakening public opinion to prepare the public mind for yet another U.S. Supreme Court decision—a successor to the *Dred Scott* decision that would use the same constitutional doctrines to spread the institution of slavery into the free states. Lincoln's speech was extremely charismatic:

If this principle is established, that there is no wrong in slavery, and whoever wants it has a right to have it, is a matter of dollars and cents, a sort of question as to how they shall deal with brutes, that between us and the negro here there is no sort of question, but that at the South the question is between the negro and the crocodile . . . where this doctrine prevails, the miners and sappers will have formed public opinion for the slave trade. They will be ready for Jeff. Davis and [Alexander] Stephens and the other leaders of that company, to sound the

bugle for the revival of the slave trade, for the second Dred
Scott decision, for the flood of slavery to be poured over the
free States, while we shall be here tied down and helpless and
run over like sheep.[3]

Douglas, said Lincoln, was subverting America by reducing fellow
human beings—blacks—to the status of beasts, not only as a *fact*
in the slave-holding South but in the culture of ideas that governed
public opinion all over the United States: "Did you ever five years
ago, hear of anybody in the world saying that the negro had no share
in the Declaration of National Independence; that it did not mean
negroes at all; and when 'all men' were spoken of negroes were not
included? . . . I have been unable at any time to find a man in an
audience who would declare that he had ever known any body saying so five years ago. But last year there was not a Douglas popular
sovereign in Illinois who did not say it."[4]

Was this true in Ohio, Lincoln asked. Perhaps many a man in the
audience "declares his firm belief that the Declaration of Independence did not mean negroes at all," but how many had believed such
a thing only five years before? Something had changed: the whole
country was being subverted, Lincoln said, by a new and barbaric
transformation. The negro was being dehumanized, reduced to a
beast, another species, a brute:

> If you think that now, and did not think it then, the next
> thing that strikes me is to remark that there has been a *change*
> wrought in you (laughter and applause), and a very significant
> change it was, being no less than changing the negro, in your
> estimation, from the rank of a man to that of a brute. They are
> taking him down, and placing him, when spoken of, among
> reptiles and crocodiles, as Judge Douglas himself expresses
> it. . . . I ask you to note that fact, and the like of which is to
> follow, to be plastered on, layer after layer, until very soon you
> are prepared to deal with the negro everywhere as with the
> brute. If public sentiment has not been debauched already to
> this point, a new turn of the screw in that direction is all that
> is wanting. (original emphasis)[5]

Lincoln was furious—furious with racists who would choke the human conscience with layers of "plaster," plastering over our decent feelings with layers of ridiculous and vicious ideology. Douglas was dehumanizing whites as well as blacks, Lincoln said: Douglas was turning Northern whites from the ways of moral decency to icy and immoral indifference.

Question: is it likely that a gut-level bigot would address his fellow whites in this manner? Would a bigot lash out at the race ideologists with such moral passion and fury? Would it not be an *enemy* of racists who could speak of "debauching" the public with the Douglas "crocodile" theory—an enemy of racists who could speak of a plaster-like veneer that was smothering natural feelings, humanitarian feelings?

Or was Lincoln attacking *his own* inner bigotry—in secret? If the Huck Finn theory is correct, Lincoln's better side was starting to prevail over gut-level notions of race. But does the theory of a bigoted Lincoln really make sense to us now—does it make any gut-level sense—when we hear Lincoln saying that *instinctively* (way down deep) we know that other races are human unless a vile *change* has been instilled in us by something external and alien? Until external applications of a vile and stupid ideology (layers of plaster) have smothered our intuitive connection with other human beings?

By the standards of the master-politician theory, the Columbus speech is quite significant. Lincoln's strategy was changing in 1859: he was testing how far he might go in attacking race theory aggressively. He was taking new risks in Columbus.

Just after he delivered this fiery address, a resident of Ohio asked him about racial intermarriage: he was asked to share his observations in regard to the Illinois law that forbade it. Here is Lincoln's answer, set forth in the account of the man who asked him the question: "The law means nothing. I shall never marry a negress, but I have no objection to any one else doing so. If a white man wants to marry a negro woman, let him do it—*if the negro woman can stand it*" (original emphasis).[6]

"THE NIGGER" IN THE WOODPILE.

"'The Nigger' in the Woodpile," anti-Lincoln cartoon by Currier and Ives published in 1860. A racist objects when both Lincoln and Horace Greeley try to calm him down as he attacks the Republican platform. Greeley says, "I assure you, my friend, that you can safely vote our ticket, for we have no connection with the Abolition party, but our Platform is composed entirely of rails, split by our candidate." The racist replies, "It's no use, old fellow! You can't pull that wool over my eyes, for I can see 'the Nigger' peeping through the rails." Lincoln comments, "Little did I think when I split these rails that they would be the means of elevating me to my present position." This drawing is attributed to Louis Maurer. Library of Congress.

"Miscegenation, or the Millennium of Abolitionism," racist cartoon attacking Lincoln in 1864. A black woman, presented to Lincoln by U.S. Senator Charles Sumner, says, "Dont do nuffin now but gallevant 'round wid de white gemmen!" A white woman embraces a black man and says, "Oh! You dear creature. I am so agitated! Go and ask Pa." An Irishwoman pushes a baby carriage with a black infant and laments, "And is it to drag naggur babies that I left old Ireland?" A German observer says, "Mine Got. Vat a guntry, vat a beebles!" Bromley and Company deposited the print in July 1864 for copyright. Library of Congress.

"Emancipation," print by Thomas Nast depicting the outrages of slavery contrasted to the prospects for liberation, with an oval portrait of Lincoln bottom center. Library of Congress.

"Abraham Lincoln and Sojourner Truth, 1864." This painting depicts the meeting in October 1864 between Lincoln and the black abolitionist Sojourner Truth at the White House. Lincoln is showing her the Bible that a delegation of free blacks from Baltimore presented to him on September 7. Sojourner Truth said that she "never was treated by any one with more kindness and cordiality than was shown me by that great and good man." Painted by John S. Jackson after Frank C. Courter, 1915, oil on canvas. Detroit Historical Society.

EMANCIPATION, COLONIZATION, AND
THE EQUAL RIGHTS POSSIBILITY

The election of Lincoln to the presidency triggered the Civil War: the leaders of the slave states reacted right away.

They refused to let Lincoln and his fellow Republicans shut them out of the West. Their reasoning was simple: with slavery contained, the free states would dominate the slave states by super-majority dimensions in another few decades. Then the free-state majority would use all the power of the federal government to terminate or phase out slavery.

So secession began, and the newly elected president was determined to stop it.

But his new responsibilities forced a new caution when it came to both slavery and race. For Lincoln knew that the Democrats—a proslavery party since the Kansas-Nebraska schism—would claim that the Republicans caused an unnecessary war because their Free Soil platform had pushed the South over the brink. And the threat of an antiwar, white-supremacist backlash would dog Lincoln's heels until the very last months of his presidency. He had to keep the Democrats from capturing control of Congress—at all costs.

So he emphasized patriotic Unionism, and he tried to de-emphasize slavery, at least for a time. But he never retreated from his Free Soil pledge, and he even tried to start the next phase of his antislavery program: the phase-out. He had to begin very quietly; he had to use the lofty rhetoric of war as his excuse to extend his antislavery agenda.

The Confederates were anything but quiet when it came to slavery and race. Confederate Vice President Alexander Stephens used scientific racism to justify destroying the Union. In the famous/infamous "cornerstone" speech that he delivered in Savannah, Georgia, on March 21, 1861, he declared that the Confederacy

> has put at rest forever all the agitating questions relating to our peculiar institution—African slavery as it exists among us—the proper status of the negro in our form of civilization. This was the immediate cause of the late rupture and present revolution. Jefferson, in his forecast, had anticipated this, as the "rock upon which the old Union would split." He was right. . . . But . . . the prevailing ideas entertained by him and most of the leading statesmen at the time of the formation of the old Constitution were, that the enslavement of the African was in violation of the laws of nature. . . . Those ideas, however, were fundamentally wrong. They rested upon an assumption of the equality of the races. This was an error. . . . Our new Government is founded upon exactly the opposite ideas; its foundations are laid, its cornerstone rests, upon the great truth that the negro is not equal to the white man; that slavery, subordination to the superior race, is his natural and moral condition. This, our new Government, is the first, in the history of the world, based upon this great physical, philosophical, and moral truth.[1]

According to Stephens, the Confederates were champions of progress by founding their government on racist doctrine. Across the Atlantic Ocean, there were others (Count Gobineau in France, for example) who were starting to proclaim the "great truth" that only race should determine modern politics. In Germany—as the scholarship of George L. Mosse made clear long ago—the intellectual sources of National Socialism were seething.[2] Confederate nationhood could have had a horrific effect upon the modern world: it could have served as the great racist prototype.

The Confederates projected their racial theories across the Atlantic quickly in their bid to attract foreign allies. A key figure in the effort was Henry Hotze, a Swiss-born writer who had come to the United States and espoused racism. He liked what he saw in the South. He translated Gobineau's *Essai sur l'inegalité des Races Humaines* into English. And the Confederates sent him to London to agitate on their behalf. He founded the *Index*, a pro-Confederate journal that developed significant influence.[3] Certain people in Britain were receptive; a scientific writer named Richard Owen gave a lecture in 1861 entitled "The Gorilla and the Negro." Owen argued that blacks, though human in a limited sense, were very close to a degraded subspecies.[4] Another British racist, Dr. James Hunt, formed the Anthropological Society of London in 1863 as a vehicle for advancing the "polygenist" argument that Africans were a distinct and inferior species.[5]

The illustrious Charles Darwin found the racist hypothesis repulsive.[6] It also bears noting that the racists lost a powerful spokesman in June 1861: Stephen Douglas dropped dead.

In any case, Lincoln began to develop a stealthy emancipation strategy. In November 1861, he tried to start a secret program that he hoped would induce the legislature in the tiny slave state of Delaware to *ask* for federal funding to rid their state of the evil. As he did this, certain abolitionists complained about his cautious ways. They urged him to be bold and to extend the aims of war beyond the goal of preserving the Union.[7]

Early in 1862, he made off-the-record statements (if surviving accounts are to be believed) that fit the theory of the master politician so well that the accounts deserve to be presented. Consider what he said (allegedly) to two abolitionists, William Ellery Channing and Moncure Daniel Conway, in January 1862. The source for this account is the autobiography of Conway.

If Conway was telling the truth (and remembering correctly), Lincoln joked about the clever and deceptive ways in which a good cause could work sub rosa. Channing began the discussion by declaring "his belief that the opportunity of the nation to rid itself of slavery had arrived." Lincoln asked him to be more specific, so "Channing suggested emancipation with compensation for the slaves." Lincoln "said he had for years been in favour of that plan." Then Conway turned to Lincoln and asked whether "the masses of the American people would hail you as their deliverer if, at the end of this war, the Union should be surviving and slavery still in it." Lincoln said that they might "if they were to see that slavery was on the downhill."

But then Lincoln said that other methods—devious methods— might be used to help the liberating process. He made a joke about the "dry" (prohibitionist) state of Maine to express his point by way of metaphor: "I think the country grows in this direction daily, and I am not without hope that something of the desire of you and your friends may be accomplished. Perhaps it may be in the way suggested by a thirsty soul in Maine who found he could only get liquor from a druggist; as his robust appearance forbade the plea of sickness, he called for a soda, and whispered, 'Couldn't you put a drop o' the creeter into it unbeknownst to yourself?'"[8]

Here was a joke about deniability; Lincoln might find a way to "spike the soda," adding stronger antislavery measures to the war "unbeknownst to himself," as if he didn't have the faintest idea of what his right hand and left hand were doing.

This is second-hand evidence, of course, and the account is derived from an autobiography published in 1904. So one needs to ask the question directly: can we *know* that Conway was telling the truth about Lincoln and his pointed little joke? Not for a fact—and yet the likelihood that Conway was telling the truth is increased by the fact that another abolitionist, Wendell Phillips, wrote that Lincoln had told him the very same joke only sixty days after the meeting with Conway and Channing.[9]

Lincoln's deception was to use the patriotic side of the war to support him as he undermined slavery. He would claim that stronger antislavery measures might save the Union and that *only* the motive of saving the Union had been prompting him to think in this manner. In a famous public letter that he wrote to the Republican editor Horace Greeley in August 1862, Lincoln claimed that "my paramount object in this war *is* to save the Union, and is *not* either to save or to destroy slavery" (original emphasis).[10]

This was nonsense. And the nonsense has continued to convince, for surely millions believe that the Emancipation Proclamation was exactly what Lincoln proclaimed it to be: a measure for saving the

Union and shortening the war. But the deceptive nature of Lincoln's claim can be demonstrated several ways. First, it raised the question of what had initially caused the war, for no breach in the Union would have happened if Lincoln had retreated from his Free Soil pledge in the latter months of 1860. A compromise measure in Congress to pre-empt secession by allowing the expansion of slavery (the Crittenden compromise) was derailed by Lincoln, who instructed Republicans to kill it. If Lincoln only wanted to save the Union, then he should have supported this compromise.

But he didn't.

Second, there were other ways to save the Union, not least of all the method of the Peace Democrats or Copperheads, who called for negotiations with the South to restore the Union on distinctly proslavery terms. Lincoln ignored such proposals. So his paramount object was *not* to save the Union in a manner indifferent to slavery— he had after all *attacked* Stephen Douglas for saying that he didn't care about slavery—but to save it in a way that would force the evil "downhill," to cite the phrase from Conway's account.

This had always been his paramount objective. But with Democrats playing the race card—complaining that Republican "negro lovers" had caused an unnecessary war—Lincoln had to be crafty indeed.

His attempt to expand the Union war aims through positive per-suasion came to naught in the early months of 1862. His offer of funding to states that would begin to get rid of slavery—Republicans had pushed it through Congress in March 1862—had no effect at all; not a single state applied for these funds. And when Republicans passed a limited emancipation measure (the second Confiscation Act, passed in July) that would free the slaves of masters who were proven to be aiding the Confederacy, a white-racist reaction in the North began. Riots against free blacks broke out in Northern cities. One New York newspaper ran the following headline: "Can Niggers Conquer Americans?" Congressman George Julian of Indiana, a Radical Republican, wrote that "our people hate the Negro with a perfect if not a supreme hatred."[11]

So Lincoln worked up a different plan in the summer of 1862—a plan to free *all* the slaves in the *rebel states* (as opposed to the loyal slave states) using military necessity as the legal (and political) rationale. He had to find "cover" to prevent the white-supremacist backlash from worsening.

The preliminary Emancipation Proclamation of Lincoln went far beyond the Radical Republicans' second Confiscation Act. The latter freed slaves if they could prove that their masters were rebels. But Lincoln eliminated this burden of proof in his great proclamation. He said he would free *all* the slaves in rebel states (or portions of states) where rebellion was continuing as of January 1, 1863.

The famous preliminary proclamation that Lincoln would issue on September 22, 1862, was therefore a *warning* to rebels to lay down their arms by the end of the year or else forfeit their slaves. Lincoln was prepared, if the war continued, to issue the second and definitive proclamation on New Year's Day 1863.

But he was fearful of the white-supremacist reaction, especially if he tipped his hand before the midterm elections of November. His emancipation announcement could play into the Democrats' hands and give them control of Congress.

In August he attempted to show the white supremacists that striking down slavery was nothing to be feared: he would demonstrate the feasibility of "colonizing" liberated slaves in some other country. An Indiana politician told Lincoln that colonization "will, if adopted, relieve the free states of the apprehension now prevailing, and fostered by the disloyal, that they are to be overrun by negroes made free by war."[12]

This opinion was widespread in Republican circles. On July 16, a congressional committee recommended spending $20 million on colonization because of "the opposition of a large portion of our people to the intermixture of the races. . . . This is a question of color, and is unaffected by the relation of master and slave." According to this report, the "most formidable difficulty [facing] emancipation" was "the belief, which obtains especially among those who own no slaves, that if the negroes shall become free, they must still continue in our midst, and, so remaining after their liberation, they may in some measure be made equal to the Anglo-Saxon race."[13]

On August 14, Lincoln had a long meeting at the White House with five free blacks from the District of Columbia. The meeting with this delegation had been organized by James Mitchell, a Methodist minister who had worked with the American Colonization Society. Lincoln's remarks were recorded by a journalist. This was the very first time that any blacks had been invited to the White House except in the capacity of servants and cooks.

"Your race," Lincoln told his black visitors, "are suffering, in my judgment, the greatest wrong inflicted on any people. . . . On this broad continent, not a single man of your race is made the equal of a single man of ours." And this, Lincoln said, was "a fact, about which we all think and feel alike, I and you." But it was "a fact with which we have to deal . . . [for] I cannot alter it."

Lincoln actually told his black guests—on the record—that he *shared their feelings* in regard to white supremacy. Was this statement of Lincoln's sincere? If not, he was taking a significant risk, for a journalist was writing down his words.

Lincoln continued: the "unwillingness on the part of our people, harsh as it may be, for you free colored people to remain with us" suggested that a nucleus of free blacks might consider—as an influential demonstration—the chance of starting life over in a country that was less encumbered by bigotry. A successful experiment along these lines might "open a wide door for many to be made free." For a vanguard of emigrants, if gifted with the spirit of adventure, could render white antagonism moot; they would demonstrate a way in which the races could go their separate ways in peace.

Lincoln spoke of Liberia in guarded terms as an obvious place to be considered. But he said that he also understood why Liberia might be unattractive to American blacks: "The colony of Liberia has been in existence a long time. In a certain sense it is a success. . . . The question is if the colored people are persuaded to go anywhere, why not there? One reason for an unwillingness to do so is that some of you would rather remain within reach of the country of your nativity. I do not know how much attachment you may have toward our race. It does not strike me that you have the greatest reason to love them."

Still, said Lincoln, if Africa seemed too distant, he knew of a place in Central America "that has all the advantages for a colony." Lincoln was referring to a tract in the Chiriqui province of Panama (still a part of Colombia at the time) that a speculator, Ambrose Thompson, had been trying to sell to the U.S. government. "I shall," Lincoln said, "if I get a sufficient number of you engaged, have provisions made that you shall not be wronged."

Lincoln said that the place he had in mind was apparently rich in coal. "Why I attach so much importance to coal is, it will afford an opportunity to the inhabitants for immediate employment till they get ready to settle permanently in their homes. . . . If something is started so that you can get your daily bread as soon as you reach there, it is a great advantage." Most important, Lincoln said, "I would endeavor to have you made equals" with the Latin American inhabitants "and have the best assurance that you should be the equals of the best."[14]

Lincoln made it clear in his remarks that any colonization would have to be voluntary to have his presidential support.

The chairman of the black delegation, Edward M. Thomas, told Lincoln a few days later that the speech had converted him from opposition to colonization to active support. Thomas, who headed an Anglo African Institute for the Encouragement of Industry and Art, was not alone: Congress had received a petition from 242 blacks in California who expressed their desire to move to some country where their color would not be "a badge of degradation." Just four years earlier, some blacks in New York led by Henry Highland Garnet had created the African Civilization Society to encourage black support for emigration. But other blacks found the prospect insulting, and they communicated their feelings to Lincoln. Among the most contemptuous critics of Lincoln at the time was Frederick Douglass.[15]

In any case, by mid-September, five hundred blacks had signed up for Lincoln's colonization experiment, and four thousand more were on the waiting list. But the Chiriqui project was shelved in October due to several developments: Lincoln's ongoing efforts to ascertain both the validity of Thompson's claim to the land and the actual value of the coal deposits—their value had been questioned by Joseph Henry of the Smithsonian Institution—began leading him to conclude that the Panama project was a swindle. Moreover, the governments of Nicaragua, Costa Rica, San Salvador, Guatemala, Brazil, and Honduras had protested against the project.[16]

Lincoln had assured the free blacks in his White House speech that "to your colored race" the inhabitants of Central America "have no objection." It seemed by October as if that conjecture could well have been mistaken.

But the colonization experiment continued on an island off the coast of Haiti: Ile-a-Vache. Black advocates of colonization had been working with the government of Haiti for several years. On December 31, 1862, Lincoln signed a contract with a New York businessman named Bernard Kock to resettle up to five thousand free blacks on Ile-a-Vache. Kock proved unreliable, so Lincoln canceled his contract in April 1863. Then some New York financiers who had been backers of Kock—Paul S. Forbes and Charles K. Tuckerman—offered Lincoln to fulfill the original commitment. Lincoln gave them the go-ahead to proceed.[17]

Thus in 1863, the U.S. government assisted some blacks who wished to leave America and head for what appeared to be more hospitable shores.

So much for colonization as a factor in Lincoln's emancipation policy. But before the end of 1862, Lincoln started to consider the alternative of equal rights in America. After all, he had insisted that the colonization of blacks had to be voluntary: there would be no "deportation" under Lincoln. That being the case, it stood to reason he would have to consider the plight of free blacks who chose to stay.

And so he did. He began with his tried-and-true modus operandi: by softening public opinion. In his message to Congress of December 1, 1862, Lincoln started to argue with racists again: not just about slavery, as he did in the 1850s, but about the real prospect of living side by side with free blacks as American neighbors. Here is yet another Lincoln statement on race that deserves much-greater attention than it usually receives.

Racists, wrote Lincoln, were afraid that all the newly emancipated blacks—and Lincoln was drafting his definitive Emancipation Proclamation that would take effect on New Year's Day—"will swarm forth, and cover the whole land." But "are they not already in the land?" If all the blacks residing in the nation, both north and south, were "distributed among the whites of the whole country . . . there would be but one colored to seven whites," Lincoln pointed out. Then he took the big plunge: "there are many communities now having more than one free colored person, to seven whites, and this, without any apparent consciousness of evil from it."[18]

Lincoln was writing in favorable terms about racial integration. The real challenge, Lincoln wrote, in regard to the problem of slavery and race was a simple proposition in humanitarian terms: "Can we all do better?"[19]

In 1863, Lincoln put his new emancipation policy to work: thousands of slaves were set free in the South and especially in Mississippi in the aftermath of Grant's successful Vicksburg campaign.

The racist outcry was enormous. But Lincoln strove to counteract the backlash in any way he could. For one thing, he gave the freed slaves (adult males, at least) a chance to serve in the U.S. Army and fight for the Union. Congress had already provided for this possibility in the second Confiscation Act, but it was up to the commander-in-chief to make the operational decision. Lincoln did so in 1863. And he used the force of patriotic sentiment to portray these blacks as saviors of the Union.

On March 26, he wrote to Andrew Johnson, a former senator and Tennessee Unionist, who was serving as the occupation governor: "The colored population is the great *available* and yet *unavailed of,* force for restoring the Union. The bare sight of fifty thousand armed, and drilled Black soldiers on the banks of the Mississippi, would end the rebellion at once" (original emphasis).[20]

After blacks won distinction in the battles of Port Hudson, Louisiana, and Fort Wagner, South Carolina, Lincoln seized the opportunity to shame white supremacists—to try to make them feel like cowards and traitors—for maligning the blacks who put their lives on the line for their country. On August 26, he sent a long public letter to a friend of his in Springfield, Illinois—James C. Conkling—with instructions to pass it along to the newspapers.

In this letter Lincoln made clear what he thought of white supremacists who criticized his "negro-loving" ways: "To be plain, you are dissatisfied with me about the negro. Quite likely there is a difference of opinion between you and myself upon that subject.

I certainly wish that all men could be free, while I suppose you do not. . . . You say you will not fight to free negroes. Some of them seem willing to fight for you. . . ." By the end of the letter, Lincoln's anger had become intense: "Peace does not appear so distant as it did. I hope it will come soon, and come to stay; and so come as to be worth the keeping in all future time. . . . And then, there will be some black men who can remember that, with silent tongue, and clenched teeth, and steady eye, and well-poised bayonet, they have helped mankind on to this great consummation, while, I fear, there will be some white ones, unable to forget that, with malignant heart, and deceitful speech, they have strove to hinder it."[21]

In the same month, Frederick Douglass paid a call upon Lincoln. Initially a critic of Lincoln, Douglass found himself stunned by the Emancipation Proclamation; he could see "in its spirit," he wrote, "a life and power far beyond its letter. Its meaning to me was the entire abolition of slavery, wherever the evil could be reached by the Federal arm, and I saw that its moral power would extend much further."[22]

Douglass called upon Lincoln to request equal treatment for the blacks who were serving in uniform. "I was induced to go to Washington," he recalls in his autobiography, "and lay the complaints of my people before President Lincoln and the secretary of war; and to urge upon them such action as should secure to the colored troops then fighting for the country, a reasonable degree of fair play." Douglass thought long and hard about the implications of a black man calling at the White House uninvited: "The distance then between the black man and the white American citizen, was immeasurable. . . . I was an ex-slave, identified with a despised race; and yet I was to meet the most exalted person in this great republic. . . . I could not know what kind of a reception would be accorded me. I might be told to go home and mind my business . . . or I might be refused an interview altogether."[23]

But Douglass was admitted to an interview with Lincoln on August 10. And he remembered ever afterward that Lincoln's "strong face . . . lighted up as soon as my name was mentioned. As I approached and was introduced to him, he rose and extended his hand, and bade me welcome." Douglass recalls, "I was never more quickly or more completely put at ease in the presence of a great man than in that of Abraham Lincoln. . . . In his company I was never in any way reminded of my humble origin or of my unpopular color."[24]

Lincoln asked Douglass to share his complaints about the treatment of the new black troops. So Douglass got down to business:

> I replied that there were three particulars which I wished to bring to his attention. First, that colored soldiers ought to receive the same wages as those paid to white soldiers. Second, that colored soldiers ought to receive the same protection when taken prisoners, and be exchanged as readily, and on the same terms, as any other prisoners, and if Jefferson Davis should shoot or hang colored soldiers in cold blood, the United States government should retaliate in kind and degree. . . . Third, when colored soldiers seeking the "bauble-reputation at the cannon's mouth," performed great and uncommon service on the battlefield, they would be rewarded by distinction and promotion.[25]

Lincoln, according to Douglass, "listened with patience and silence to all I had to say. He was serious and even troubled by what I had said, and by what he had evidently thought himself before on the same points." Then Lincoln replied. "He began by saying that the employment of colored troops at all was a great gain to the colored people; that the measure could not have been successfully adopted at the beginning of the war; that the wisdom of making colored men into soldiers was still doubted; and that their enlistment was a serious offense to popular prejudice . . . that the fact that they were not to receive the same pay as white soldiers, seemed a necessary concession to smooth the way to their employment at all as soldiers; but that ultimately they would receive the same."[26]

To Douglass, Lincoln said, in effect, that he would "smooth the way" to equal treatment for the blacks in uniform. As to black promotions, he deferred to the secretary of war. And as to retaliation for Confederate war crimes, Lincoln said he was averse to responding to racist brutality with counterbrutality.[27]

In 1863, he took further action to upgrade the social status of blacks who chose to stay in America. Congress in the previous year had levied a direct tax, a tax upon everyone, including the rebels, who—since secession was held to be illegal and thus null and void—could be regarded as being U.S. citizens regardless of their claims to be citizens of the Confederate States. And if the rebels failed to pay what they owed to Uncle Sam, they could forfeit their real estate: a handy pretext for social revolution in the South through the confiscation of rebel plantations.

The confiscation began in the Sea Islands off the coast of South Carolina, which Union troops had managed to occupy. In 1863, Lincoln dashed off orders to ensure that some of this confiscated land would be set aside for former slaves—specifically, twenty-acre lots for "heads of families of the African race, one only to each, preferring such as by their good conduct, meritorious services or exemplary character, will be examples of moral propriety and industry."[28]

Lincoln also wrote an old friend of his, Stephen A. Hurlbut, who was serving as a Union general in occupied Mississippi. Lincoln expressed great concern about the fate of the liberated slaves and especially the women and children: while "the able bodied male contrabands [former slaves] are already employed by the Army," Lincoln wrote, the others were possibly living "in confusion and destitution." Lincoln told his friend to make use of abandoned plantations, putting "as many contrabands on such, as they will hold—that is, as can draw subsistence from them. If some still remain, get loyal men, of character in the vicinity, to take them temporarily on wages, to be paid to the contrabands themselves—such men obliging themselves to not let the contrabands be kidnapped, or forcibly taken away. Of course, if any voluntarily make arrangements to work for their living, you will not hinder them."[29]

Lincoln was preoccupied with winning the war before he had to face the voters in election year 1864. He was fearful that a white-supremacist Democrat would throw him out of office and reverse the emancipation policy. Military victory was vital to avert this scenario.

But Lincoln wrote a stunning private memo during 1863—a memo in which he expressed his fear about the *wrong kind* of military victory. He insisted on saving the Union *his way*, with all the progress for blacks protected from a counterrevolution. This astonishing memorandum deserves to be quoted:

Suppose those now in rebellion should say: "We cease fighting: re-establish the national authority among us—customs, courts, mails, land-offices,—all as before the rebellion—we claiming to send members to both branches of Congress, as of yore, and to hold our slaves according to our State laws, notwithstanding anything or all things which has [*sic*] occurred during the rebellion." I shall dread, and I think we all should dread, to see "the disturbing element" so brought back into the government. . . . During my continuance here, the government will return no person to slavery who is free according to the proclamation, or to any of the acts of congress, unless such return shall be held to be a legal duty, by the proper court of final resort.[30]

The proper court of final resort was the U.S. Supreme Court—still under the gavel of Chief Justice Roger B. Taney, of *Dred Scott* infamy. And it was only a matter of time before a challenge to Lincoln's emancipation policy would arrive in court. To avert this scenario, Lincoln had suggested constitutional amendments in his annual message to Congress of December 1, 1862. But no preemptive amendments had been passed. Everything that Lincoln had achieved in racial progress might be swept away.

Even so, Lincoln tried to push matters further in 1864: he began to endorse the idea of granting voting rights to blacks incrementally. But his initial endorsement of this volatile measure was secret and for very good reason.

VOTING RIGHTS AND
LINCOLN'S MURDER

I n anticipation of worst-case possibilities, Lincoln took preemptive action in 1863 to avert an electoral catastrophe for the Republicans (and for America) in 1864. Since his hope to protect emancipation with constitutional amendments had (as yet) come to nothing, Lincoln improvised a very different strategy: he would use the advantages of military force in some occupied Confederate states to redraft their constitutions and abolish slavery.

Lincoln's secret machinations supply us with some valuable evidence regarding the master-politician theory: the theory that Lincoln was a Machiavellian strategist who outmaneuvered opponents to achieve moral ends that might otherwise have been impossible. In fact, the evidence here is so decisive that the story should be told at some length.

He began in the largely occupied state of Louisiana, where "free state" Unionists under the leadership of Thomas J. Durant, Michael Hahn, and Benjamin Flanders were interested in redrafting the state's constitution. To head them off and to protect the institution of slavery, other state leaders who claimed to be Unionists requested Lincoln to let them reestablish home rule with the existing state constitution. Lincoln told them on June 19 that since "reliable information has reached me that a respectable portion of the Louisiana people, desire to amend their State constitution . . . the general government should not give the commital you seek, to the existing State constitution."[1]

Thus began a long process that would lead, in a year, to Lincoln's secret use of the Louisiana occupation to test the possibility of phasing in voting rights for blacks.

Lincoln secretly directed his commander of the occupation forces, the political general and fellow Republican Nathaniel Banks, to work with the Louisiana free-state leaders to make the transformation happen. With nimble language, Lincoln made it very clear to Banks that the presidential hand must be concealed, completely concealed; the process should seem to be a grass-roots expression of the people's will, without intervention from the White House. On August 5 Lincoln wrote to Banks:

> While I very well know what I would be glad for Louisiana to do, it is quite a different thing for me to assume direction of the matter. I would be glad for her to make a new Constitution recognizing the emancipation proclamation, and adopting emancipation in those parts of the state to which the proclamation does not apply. . . . If these views can be of any advantage in giving shape, impetus, and action there, I shall be glad for you to use them prudently for that object. Of course you will confer with intelligent and trusty citizens of the state, among whom I would suggest Messrs. Flanders, Hahn, and Durant.[2]

Lincoln used the same strategy in occupied Tennessee but without the detachment that he chose to employ with Banks; in September he wrote to Andrew Johnson: "Not a moment should be lost. . . . Get emancipation into your new State government—Constitution— . . . [since] it can not be known who is next to occupy the position I now hold, nor what he will do."[3]

As 1863 drew to a close, Lincoln started to feel more anxiety. The Louisiana process had become bogged down, and in November Lincoln told his agent Banks that "this disappoints me bitterly. There is danger, even now, that the adverse element seeks insidiously to pre-occupy the ground." Lincoln said there was a danger that "a few professedly loyal men shall draw the disloyal about them, and colorably set up a State government, repudiating the emancipation proclamation, and re-establishing slavery." Lincoln told Banks that he should force the process ahead as quickly as possible; he should "lose no more time." There was no doubt at all that Lincoln was "assuming direction of the matter," though he had to maintain deniability.

When he sent his long annual message to Congress in December, he proposed a plan of Reconstruction: the famous 10 percent plan that was attacked very quickly by the Radical Republicans as "too lenient." Indeed, the plan is still regarded by a great many people as "lenient." What most Americans are probably taught in their history classes is that Lincoln made it easy for Confederates to stop fighting; he wanted Reconstruction to be fast. If merely 10 percent of the voting population (as of 1860) took a loyalty oath, then that minority could go right ahead and commence home rule.

A "lenient" plan, yes—except for one particular provision that is often overlooked (or not taught): Lincoln required these voters to take a second oath as well if they intended to vote. They would have to take an oath—an oath upon the holy Bible in the Bible Belt, which was a serious matter in the culture of the South—that they supported the Emancipation Proclamation and all the antislavery acts of Congress. Only *then* could they vote. In other words, the only people whom Lincoln would allow to vote in the ex-Confederate states would be opponents of slavery! And it would only take a tiny minority of such people—10 percent—to overpower proslavery majorities of up to 90 percent and transform their states into free states against the will of these racist majorities.

Here was surely a masterstroke of Machiavellian cunning: Lincoln's "lenient" plan (and it appeared so lenient to Radical Republicans that they condemned it) was in many respects *the reverse* of what Lincoln made it seem. It was a pushy and high-handed action to force the conversion of slave states into free states by presidential maneuver, assisted by a handful of local allies.

Early in 1864, Banks speeded things up by postponing the convention to redraft the state constitution of Louisiana (this particular part of the process had run into delays) and holding early elections for state offices instead: elections per the terms of Lincoln's "lenient" 10 percent plan. The result was the election of Hahn as Louisiana's "free state" governor.

Just after the election, two leaders of the free black community in New Orleans, Arnold Bertonneau and Jean-Baptiste Roudanez, came to Washington and called upon Lincoln. Like Frederick Douglass, these blacks obtained a presidential interview. They complained that they and other blacks had not been permitted to vote in the election that swept Hahn into power. Their interview with Lincoln occurred on March 12, 1864.[4] On the very next day, Lincoln wrote to Hahn: "I congratulate you on having fixed your name in history as the first free-state Governor of Louisiana. Now you are about to have a Convention which, among other things, will probably define the elective franchise. . . . I barely suggest for your private consideration, whether some of the colored people may not be let in—as, for instance, the very intelligent, and especially those who have fought gallantly in our ranks. . . . But this is only a suggestion, not to the public, but to you alone."[5]

Not to the public: is there any reason for doubting any longer that Lincoln was the sort of politician who would work behind the scenes and use deception to advance black interests?

Perhaps a note about voting rights is necessary here: when Lincoln spoke of the "elective franchise," he spoke about a matter that was still the exclusive constitutional prerogative of the states. In colonial times, the "elective franchise" had varied from one English colony to another. And this tradition continued in the early American nation: voting rights were determined by the states and the states alone. And nothing could be taken for granted; even *adult white males* could not vote automatically in some of the states. They were subjected to a number of requirements in several states: property requirements and literacy tests, in particular.[6]

Even the Fifteenth Amendment to the Constitution (1870)—the amendment that is often in historical shorthand regarded as the document that "gave" blacks the right to vote—left the states' constitutional authority intact, with the exception of a few stipulations. The Fifteenth Amendment proclaims, in part, that "the right of the citizens of the United States to vote shall not be denied or abridged by the United States or by any State on account of race, color, or previous condition of servitude." This, of course, left the states quite free to deny voting rights for other reasons such as poverty (inability to pay a poll tax) or illiteracy (inability to pass a literacy test). Only with the passage of the 1965 Voting Rights Act would such state shenanigans be curbed through federal action.

Regardless, the states remained the arbiters of voting rights in 1864 when Lincoln recommended that blacks should be allowed to vote in Louisiana "on account of" certain factors such as military service and "intelligence," if not complete literacy. And this, we might note, was the man who told the Illinois voters in 1858 that he had "no purpose to introduce political and social equality between the white and black races." Yet, he never committed himself in the Lincoln-Douglas debates to maintain that position in the future! This lawyer had left himself a loophole. And he *did* have the "purpose" by 1864, but it had to remain at first a *hidden* purpose, a secret ("not to the public, but to you alone").

It also bears noting that Lincoln had just brought his long experiment with colonization to an end; an investigation had determined that the free black colonists were neglected on Ile-a-Vache, and so Lincoln sent a vessel to bring the survivors home. He never pushed any further schemes of colonization in public (though he might have kept the option open for blacks who desired emigration in the future); instead, his policy from that point onward was uplift for blacks right here in America, at least to the extent that the political realities permitted it.

His major policy initiative in 1864 was the Thirteenth Amendment to the Constitution, the amendment to abolish the evil of slavery forever, all over America. Lincoln insisted that this measure be inserted in the Republican Party's platform.[7] The Senate passed the amendment, but the Democrats bottled it up in the House of Representatives.

Lincoln did have the pleasure of signing some bills that permitted blacks to testify in federal courts and raised the pay for black troops, thus fulfilling the pledge to Frederick Douglass.[8] And he behaved very cordially to four daring blacks who took the chance of attending the public reception at the White House on New Year's Day in 1864.[9]

The counterattack upon Lincoln by the white supremacists was well underway in preparation for November 1864. In December 1863, an anonymous pamphlet was published and distributed in New York City: *Miscegenation: The Theory of the Blending of the Races, Applied to the American White Man and Negro*. The pamphlet appeared to be a broadside for racial equality. It advocated racial intermarriage and interracial sex—it bears noting that the new term *miscegenation* would gradually replace the older term *amalgamation*—and copies of the pamphlet were distributed to prominent Republicans with cover letters that requested their opinions and endorsements.

This was a trick: the pamphlet was written by a pair of racist Democrats, the journalists David Goodman and George Wakeman of the *New York World*.[10] They were using this hoax to get as many Republicans as possible on record, *in writing*, in support of interracial sex. They were preparing a political slaughter.

Everything began to go wrong for the Republicans and Lincoln in the spring and summer of 1864. Ulysses S. Grant's campaign against Robert E. Lee had led to stalemate—a protracted siege of Petersburg, below Richmond, that devolved into grinding trench warfare—and the casualties were appalling. War weariness began to pervade the North. And Republicans started to defect from the leadership of Lincoln. Some even called for peace negotiations with Jefferson Davis.

Against this background, a mood of triumphalism reigned among the white-supremacist Democrats. Their vilification of Lincoln was drenched in racial hatred: Democratic editors reviled the "negro-loving, negro-hugging worshippers of old Abe." One Democratic editorial went so far as to proclaim that "Abe Lincoln—passing the question as to his taint of Negro blood . . . is altogether an imbecile. . . . He is brutal in all his habits. . . . He is filthy. He is obscene. . . . He is an animal!"[11] He was caricatured as "Abraham Africanus the First," the "original ourang-outang."[12] One Democratic cartoon depicted a "Miscegenation Ball" at which white men and black women danced. The caption claimed that this dance had taken place at the "Headquarters of the Lincoln Central Campaign Club."[13] Anonymous pamphlets with titles like "The Miscegenation Record of the Republican Party" and "Miscegenation, the Millennium of Abolitionism" made the rounds in the autumn of 1864.

Some race abuse arrived at the White House. Lincoln answered with tongue-in-cheek ridicule. When one correspondent tried to argue that whites were the "first-class" people of the country, Lincoln had a secretary answer the critic and inquire if he happened to be black or white (as if Lincoln did not know). Then the letter proceeded as follows: "in either case . . . you cannot be regarded as an impartial judge. It may be that you belong to a third or fourth class of *yellow* or *red* men, in which case the impartiality of your judgment would be more apparent" (original emphasis).[14]

Deeply depressed, Lincoln called Frederick Douglass to the White House. "I went most gladly," the black abolitionist recalled. When Douglass arrived, he found Lincoln approaching the point of despair: "the increasing opposition to the war, in the north, and the mad cry against it . . . alarmed Mr. Lincoln, and made him apprehensive that a peace might be forced upon him that would leave still in slavery all who had not come within our lines." So Lincoln asked Douglass to organize "a band of scouts, composed of colored men, whose business should be . . . to go into the rebel States, beyond the lines of our armies, and carry the news of emancipation, and urge the slaves to come within our boundaries." Though Douglass himself found the situation grievous, he "listened with the deepest interest and profoundest satisfaction" to Lincoln's secret proposal.[15]

But the fortunes of war—and politics—turned when General William Tecumseh Sherman's capture of Atlanta restored the morale of Northern Unionists and swept the Republicans to landslide victory in November 1864. Lincoln went to work right away to convince the outgoing Congress to pass the Thirteenth Amendment in its lame-duck session before it adjourned. He worked relentlessly behind the scenes, and his work in the course of approximately ninety days paid off when the amendment was passed by the House of Representatives in January 1865.

Then he worked to advance black interests in a wide variety of ways. When Sherman prepared to move north into the Carolinas, he issued an order—Special Field Orders No. 15—transferring a vast tract of seized plantation lands to the newly liberated slaves who had been following his army. This was a "promissory" grant that would have to be confirmed by Congress. Lincoln let this order stand (after Lincoln's death, Andrew Johnson overturned and rescinded this order).[16] In March, Lincoln signed a bill establishing a new welfare agency, the Freedmen's Bureau, on a one-year experimental basis. Among the duties of the bureau was to survey "abandoned lands" and to lease them, in forty-acre tracts, to former slaves with an option to purchase after three years.

When Lincoln took the oath of office for a second term, Frederick Douglass took the risk of showing up at the inaugural ball. Lincoln welcomed him with enthusiasm; "he exclaimed," wrote Douglass, "so that all around could hear him, 'Here comes my friend Douglass.' Taking me by the hand, he said, 'I am glad to see you.'" Lincoln addressed Douglass, "I saw you in the crowd today, listening to my inaugural address; how did you like it?" When Douglass suggested he should not take the time to "detain you with my poor opinion, when there are thousands waiting to shake hands with you," Lincoln said, "No, no, you must stop a little, Douglass; there is no man in the country whose opinion I value more than yours." Douglass called Lincoln's speech "a sacred effort."[17]

After Douglass succeeded in gaining admittance to the ball, other free blacks followed his example.[18]

When the Confederates evacuated Richmond, Lincoln visited the city on April 4, 1865. He entered the city with an escort of black troops. Ten thousand blacks lived in Richmond, and they gave him a hero's welcome. Some knelt in his presence, and he quickly bade them rise and bend the knee no longer.[19]

In the very last speech of Lincoln's life, he declared—in public—that he favored the extension of voting rights to blacks on an incremental basis. The subject of his speech was the experiment in Louisiana and its implications for a larger Reconstruction program. The president pretended he had nothing to do with the developments in Louisiana; in one of the most brazen and (in retrospect) hilarious tongue-in-cheek performances in presidential history, he said he had been "much censured for some supposed agency in setting up, and seeking to sustain, the new State Government of Louisiana. In this I have done just so much as, and no more than, the public knows."[20]

If presidential lying can be justified now and then by circumstances—and this example provides us with a case in point—Lincoln's only hope of getting away with the deception would be the knowledge that his letters to Banks and Hahn would stay hidden for a great many years (as, of course, they did). Lincoln told the crowd—he was speaking from a White House balcony on April 11, 1865—that Louisiana politics resulted from spontaneous reactions to the "ten-percent" proposal he had offered in December 1863: "When the Message of 1863, with the plan before mentioned, reached New Orleans, Gen. Banks wrote me that he was confident the people, with his military co-operation, would reconstruct, substantially on that plan. I wrote him, and some of them to try it; they tried it, and the result is known. Such only has been my agency in getting up the Louisiana government."

Lincoln turned to the political and racial implications of Louisiana's achievement. "Some twelve thousand voters in the heretofore slave state of Louisiana," he observed, had "held elections, organized a State government, adopted a free-state constitution [this had finally been drafted; it was ratified on September 5, 1864], giving the benefit of public schools equally to black and white, and empowered the Legislature to confer the elective franchise upon the colored man."

Lincoln spoke about the issue of voting rights for blacks in a tone that was charismatic. He admitted that he knew it was "unsatisfactory to some that the elective franchise is not [already] given to the colored man." Then he came out of hiding and began to reveal his big secret: "I would myself prefer that it were now conferred on the very intelligent, and on those who serve our cause as soldiers." But the real point was "not whether the Louisiana government, as it stands, is quite all that is desirable. The question is 'Would it be wiser to take it as it is, and help to improve it.'"

With enthusiasm that leaps off the page as one reads the speech today, Lincoln said that in supporting the free-state leaders of Louisiana, "we encourage the hearts, and nerve the arms of the twelve thousand to adhere to their work, and argue for it, and proselyte for it, and fight for it, and feed it, and grow it, and ripen it to complete success. The colored man, too, in seeing all united for him, is inspired with vigilance, and energy, and daring to the same end."

Lincoln seemed to be sending a very clear message to blacks: he *wanted* them to demonstrate vigilance and energy and daring in their fight to win the vote, and he would help them in the next four years.

Indeed, said Lincoln, additional radical measures might be coming. He said that while "my promise is out" in regard to the 10 percent plan, changing circumstances might oblige the American people to understand that "as bad promises are better broken than kept, I shall treat this as a bad promise and break it, whenever I shall be convinced that keeping it is adverse to the public interest." In fact, he concluded, "It may be my duty to make some new announcement to the people of the South. I am considering, and shall not fail to act, when satisfied that action will be proper."[21]

John Wilkes Booth was on the scene as the president spoke. When Lincoln had concluded, Booth turned to his accomplices—Lewis Paine and David Herold—and said, "That means nigger citizenship. Now, by God, I'll put him through. That is the last speech he will ever make."[22]

How do we know that Booth said this? When his accomplices were prosecuted for Lincoln's murder—Booth himself, of course, was killed before he could be captured and tried—they talked to attorneys both before and during their trial. And these attorneys later wrote memoirs. And this is how we know what Booth said.

It seems appropriate here to agree with the Lincoln scholar Michael Burlingame, who has recently written that "Lincoln was a martyr to black civil rights, as much as Martin Luther King and other activists who fell victim to racist violence a century later."[23]

Lincoln's speech of April 11 had had an electrifying impact on advocates of black rights. Journalist Whitelaw Reid heard the speech and wrote a few months later that Lincoln had delivered it "with all the deliberation of a grave political manifesto."[24] Transatlantic reports of the speech prompted abolitionist Moncure Daniel Conway to defend the implications of black suffrage to skeptics in London.[25]

Reid believed that Lincoln was beginning to build up support for black suffrage in the cabinet; on the day after Lincoln gave his speech, Salmon P. Chase had written to the president urging voting rights "without regard to complexion. Once I should have been . . .

contented with suffrage for the intelligent [blacks] and for those who have been soldiers; now I am convinced that universal suffrage is demanded by sound policy and impartial justice."[26] According to Reid, Lincoln read this letter on April 13, and then "he showed it to a leading member of his cabinet; and it was so well known as to have been . . . talked of among Administration leaders at Washington at the Cabinet meeting that day. . . . Mr. Lincoln's expressions in favor of the liberality toward negro citizens . . . were fuller and more emphatic" than ever before.

Indeed, "never were the hopes of the progressive loyalists of the country in Mr. Lincoln stronger," wrote Reid. "[N]ever was their confidence in him more perfect; never was the assurance that his wisdom, benevolence, and power would secure perfect protection to the rights of all men so complete, as on the day when he was lost to the Nation and to Mankind."[27]

When Lincoln's funeral procession advanced down Pennsylvania Avenue, no less than four thousand blacks marched with it. Secretary of the Navy Gideon Welles observed that there were "no truer mourners . . . than the poor sad colored people who crowded the streets, joined the procession, and exhibited their woe, bewailing the loss of him whom they regarded as a benefactor and father."

On June 1, 1865, Douglass delivered a eulogy for Lincoln in New York City. He told of a black woman weeping at the gates of the White House when she heard that Lincoln had been shot. "We have lost our Moses," she wailed, and when a passerby told her that the Lord would send another, "that may be," she replied, "but Ah! we had him."

Douglass described how blacks were won over to Lincoln—and one has to remember that Douglass himself had been a skeptic. Blacks

early caught a glimpse of the man, and from the evidence of their senses, they believed in him. They viewed him not in the light of separate individual acts, but in the light of his mission, in his manifest relation to events and in the philosophy of his statesmanship. Viewing him thus they trusted him as men are seldom trusted. They did not care what forms of expression the President adopted, whether it were justice, expedience, or military necessity, so that they see slavery abolished and liberty established in the country. . . . Under Abraham Lincoln's beneficent rule, they saw themselves being gradually lifted to the broad plain of equal manhood; under his rule, and by measures approved by him, they saw gradually fading the handwriting of the ages which was against them. . . . Under his rule, they saw the Independence of Hayti and Liberia recognized, and the whole colored race steadily rising into the friendly consideration of the American people. In their broad practical common sense, they took no captious exceptions to the unpleasant incidents of their transition from slavery to freedom. All they wanted to know was that those incidents were only transitional and not permanent.

Douglass recalled that during one of his meetings with Lincoln— the one in which Lincoln asked him to organize "scouts" to spread the word about emancipation—an assistant to the president kept telling him that others were waiting to see him, including the governor of Connecticut. "Tell the Governor to wait," said Lincoln in Douglass's account. "I want to have a long talk with my friend Douglass." Douglass observed that "this was probably the first time in the history of our country when the Governor of a State was required to wait for an interview, because the President of the United States was engaged in conversation with a negro."

In all, Douglass said, Lincoln was "emphatically the black man's president . . . the first to show any respect for their rights as men."[28] He was emphatically the "black man's president."

DISPUTED OR DOUBTFUL EVIDENCE

Several documents pertaining to Lincoln and race are of doubtful reliability. But they should still be mentioned.

One of them is a letter attributed to Lincoln. This piece of correspondence or alleged correspondence is supposed to have been sent by Lincoln to General James S. Wadsworth circa January 1864. In the letter, Lincoln justifies the granting of voting rights to blacks, but the text's authenticity was subject to dispute a half century ago.[1] The original letter, if Lincoln really wrote it, does not survive. The text of the supposed letter that was published in Lincoln's *Collected Works* was derived (for the most part) from a version that was printed in the *New York Tribune* on September 26, 1865. Several paragraphs of this text appear to be of dubious authenticity.

In contrast to this document is the reminiscence of Ward Hill Lamon, Lincoln's friend and sometime bodyguard, who recalled that Lincoln told him on one occasion that "the question of universal suffrage to the freedman in his unprepared state is one of doubtful propriety." Though Lincoln, in Lamon's account, admitted he did not dispute "the justice of the measure," he feared that it "would redound like a boomerang not only on the Republican party but upon the freedman himself and our common country."[2]

Bearing in mind the crucial qualifying language—"universal suffrage to the freedman *in his unprepared state*" (my emphasis)—it is possible that Lincoln shared some thoughts of this type with Lamon or with others, since his plans for advancing black suffrage depended on the strategy of phasing in the measure, beginning with blacks who were "qualified."

It is equally possible, however, that Lincoln was playing devil's advocate to test the reactions to a program of "universal suffrage." He had used this tactic on other occasions—in the months before he issued the Emancipation Proclamation, for example. On September 13, 1862—with the proclamation already drafted and waiting in his desk drawer—he pretended to a group of abolitionists that he was still in doubt about it. He talked to them this way: "What *good* would a proclamation of emancipation from me do . . . ? Would *my* word free the slaves, when I cannot even enforce the Constitution in the rebel states? [And] how can we feed and care for such a multitude?" (original emphasis).[3] The artful maneuvering of Lincoln was so complex that one has to take the reminiscence of Lamon with a grain of salt.

Finally, there is the reminiscence of the political general Benjamin Butler, who claimed that as late as April 1865, Lincoln was still inclined to consider the option of colonization.[4] Some Lincoln scholars, following the lead of Mark E. Neely, are inclined to dismiss Butler's claims as fabrications.[5] Others, such as Philip W. Magness, are convinced that Butler might have told the truth, at least in part.[6]

There is reason to suppose that Lincoln could have found residual value—even after his triumphant reelection, Lee's surrender, and the imminent collapse of the Confederacy—in a program to assist free blacks who wished to leave a country whose culture of white supremacy was intolerable. After all, when he committed himself to emancipation, Lincoln started to envision new federal policies for two different free black communities: the free blacks who wished to depart from America and those who chose to stay and "tough it out."

Lincoln always liked to keep his options open. According to Butler, Lincoln feared the possibility of violence—racial violence—in the post-Confederate South. According to Butler, Lincoln said that he could "hardly believe that the South and the North can live in peace, unless we can get rid of the negro."[7]

In light of everything else that Lincoln did in the springtime of 1865, the likelihood that he said such a thing is so remote as to make Butler's paraphrase preposterous. But the prospect that Lincoln was continuing to think about extending assistance to American blacks who wished to emigrate? Yes, that is absolutely possible.

LINCOLN AND NATIVE AMERICANS

If one turns to the subject of Lincoln and Native Americans, the racial issue is complex. For in the case of blacks, Lincoln dealt with a segment of the population that was integrated in many significant ways with the patterns of mainstream American culture, notwithstanding the lingering presence of African folkways and newer subcultural patterns that shaped black American life, both among the slaves and the free.

With Native Americans, however, Lincoln faced a wide array of subcultures. Some tribes had assimilated aspects of white culture through a process of syncretism: the Cherokee were perhaps the most important example of this in the antebellum years. But other Native Americans were hostile to the "white way," and some were warlike—not only toward whites but toward other tribal groups within their own broad pattern of culture.

Nonetheless, it seems clear enough that Lincoln viewed the Native Americans as people who lived within a vastly different cultural pattern far more than he thought of them as a "race" in the genetic or biological sense. When Stephen Douglas made the racial issue so explicit—and when he pointedly included Indians and other groups within his litany of "inferior races"—Lincoln's overall response applied as much to Native Americans as it did to blacks; Lincoln found the overall emphasis on race distasteful and morally regressive.

Lincoln as president inherited an overall "Indian policy" that was rank with injustice and corruption. The long-term policies of

"Indian removal," with the "concentration" of Native Americans on reservations, had developed over many years. So had the sordid political realities of fraud and exploitation by the "Indian agents" who oversaw the different reservations. Lincoln as president was naturally preoccupied with beating the Confederates and fighting as much as he could to strike blows against the evil of slavery. But in 1862, a new "Indian war" forced the issue of Native American relations onto Lincoln's desk.

The war in question has been called by a variety of names: the Dakota War of 1862, the Sioux Rebellion of 1862, and Little Crow's War. It occurred in Minnesota, and the story is exceedingly ugly. But it was all too typical of nineteenth-century American patterns. Years of white land-grabbing, treaty violations, and other abuses had disrupted the hunting patterns that some eastern bands of Sioux or Dakota had depended upon for food. Corrupt Indian agents interfered with the federal assistance that was promised to the tribes. Violence broke out in Minnesota in the middle of August 1862. Atrocities were perpetrated on white settlers. Lincoln sent military forces under the command of General John Pope. After the Native Americans were defeated, 303 Sioux fighters were convicted of murder and rape by military tribunals and sentenced to death.

Lincoln commuted the sentences of 264 and allowed the execution of 38. This judicial outcome has been condemned as the greatest mass execution in American history. It has also been praised as the greatest single act of executive clemency in American history.[1] It bears noting that Lincoln made this decision at a time when he was dealing with a major Confederate counteroffensive, the issuance of the preliminary Emancipation Proclamation, and the crucial congressional elections of 1862.

It appears from the record that Lincoln attempted to institute reforms in the federal Indian policy that would reduce the corruption and injustice that incited such outbreaks. But his attempts were largely unsuccessful.[2]

Lincoln faced a special problem with the "Indian Territory" (future Oklahoma) since Confederates gained military power in the area and offered an alliance to the tribes—the Cherokee, Choctaw,

Seminole, and Creek—who had been sent (in reality banished) to the area before the war. The Confederate victory in the battle of Wilson's Creek on August 10, 1861, made their power preeminence daunting. Most of the aforementioned tribes signed treaties with the Confederates.

This situation was troubling for one particular Cherokee leader, Chief John Ross, who initially urged a position of neutrality. But he faced some political rivals within the tribe, notably Stand Watie, who became a Confederate general. So in August 1861, Ross abandoned his neutrality and urged a Confederate alliance.

But Lincoln decided to retake the Indian Territory, and the Union victory at Pea Ridge, Arkansas (March 6–8, 1862), changed the situation completely. Many Cherokee refugees fled to Kansas. Ross went east, in the hope of convincing Lincoln that the Cherokee had acted under duress.[3]

Ross met with Lincoln on September 12, 1862, and followed up with a letter on September 16. He told Lincoln that because of the "overwhelming pressure brought to bear upon them, the Cherokees were forced for the preservation of their Country and their existence to negotiate a treaty with the 'Confederate States.'" He asked for "all the protection in your power" to enable the Cherokee to resume their loyal relations with the federal government.[4]

Lincoln's reply was judicious and fair; he told Ross

In the multitude of cares claiming my constant attention I have been unable to examine and determine the exact treaty relations between the United States and the Cherokee Nation. Neither have I been able to investigate and determine the exact state of facts claimed by you as constituting a failure of treaty obligations on our part, excusing the Cherokee Nation for making a treaty with a portion of the people of the United States in open rebellion against the government thereof. This letter therefore, must not be understood to decide anything upon these questions. I shall, however, cause a careful investigation of them to be made. Meanwhile the Cherokee people remaining practically loyal to the federal Union will receive all the protection which can be given them consistently with the duty of the government to the whole country. I sincerely hope the Cherokee country may not again be over-run by the enemy, and I shall do all I consistently can to prevent it.[5]

The Cherokee refugees in Kansas suffered greatly, so Lincoln authorized funds for their assistance in 1864.[6] The complicated issues surrounding the Cherokee and other tribes who assisted the Confederates continued to be subjects of controversy and struggle after Lincoln's murder.

The most interesting piece of evidence concerning Lincoln's interaction with Native Americans *as people* is the meeting that he had with some tribal leaders on March 27, 1863. Leaders of the Cheyenne, Kiowai, Arapaho, Comanche, Apache, and Caddo tribes were in Washington. Lincoln arranged a reception for them in the East Room of the White House. Members of the cabinet were present, along with reporters and other Washingtonians including Joseph Henry of the Smithsonian Institution.

A press account published in the *Washington Daily Morning Chronicle* describes the scene:

> The Indian chiefs now in the city met the President of the United States and had a formal interview with him. . . . The Indians were all seated on the floor in a line, and around them the spectators formed a ring which, notwithstanding the assiduous yet polite efforts of Mr. Nicolay, was still too contracted to permit all to see the principal actors. . . . Still everything went off very well. These Indians are fine-looking men. They have all the hard and cruel lines in their faces which we might expect in savages; but they are evidently men of intelligence and force of character. They were both dignified and cordial in their manner, and listened to everything with great interest. At half past eleven the President entered the circle, and each one of the chiefs came forward and shook him by the hand, some of them adding a sort of salaam or salutation by spreading out the hands.[7]

Lincoln spoke through an interpreter, as did the chieftains. The president began by instructing the interpreter to "say to them I am very glad to see them, and if they have anything to say, it will afford me great pleasure to hear them." After listening to Lean Bear of the Cheyenne and Spotted Wolf of the Arapaho, Lincoln began his remarks with some simple observations in response to what he heard from his guests—observations that he obviously hoped would establish quick "people-to-people" rapport: "You have all spoken of the strange sights you see here, among your pale-faced brethren; the very great number of people that you see; the big wigwams; the difference between our people and your own. You may wonder when I tell you that there are people here in this wigwam, now looking at you, who have come from other countries a great deal farther off than your own."

Lincoln then began a simple geography and science lesson, making sure to present all the facts as "beliefs" or "notions" of the whites: "We pale-faced people think that this world is a great, round ball, and we have people here of the pale-faced family who have come almost from the other side of it to represent their nations here. . . . One of our learned men will now explain to you our notions about this great ball, and show you where we live."

Lincoln yielded the floor to Henry, who conducted a brief geography lesson. Then Lincoln resumed; he offered commentary on the difference between the "white way" and the "Indian way": "There is a great difference between this pale-faced people and their red brethren, both as to numbers and the way in which we live. We know not whether your own situation is best for your race, but this is what has made the difference in our way of living. The pale-faced people are numerous and prosperous because they cultivate the earth, produce bread, and depend upon the products of the earth rather than wild game for a subsistence."

Lincoln strove to maintain a stance of cultural humility while nonetheless suggesting the benefits of settled life and technological development. His choice of words was extremely significant: "You have asked for my advice. I really am not capable of advising you whether, in the providence of the Great Spirit, who is the great Father of us all, it is best for you to maintain the habits and customs of your race, or adopt a new mode of life. I can only say that I can see no way in which your race is to become as numerous and prosperous as the white race except by living as they do, by the cultivation of the earth."

Lincoln closed with some observations on the issue of white injustice and the difficulty that he faced in trying to mitigate it: "It is the object of this Government to be on terms of peace with you, and with all our red brethren. We constantly endeavor to be so. We make treaties with you, and will try to observe them; and if our children should sometimes behave badly, and violate these treaties, it is against our wish. You know it is not always possible for any father to have his children do precisely as he wishes them to do."[8]

This speech might very well be regarded by some as "paternalistic." But the case can be made that no kindlier speech could have come from the mouth of any president.

RACIST OR NOT?

The preponderance of evidence suggests that in all probability Lincoln had no racial bias. But in light of the things that Lincoln said on the record, it should not be surprising that people who otherwise disagreed completely on race—people such as James K. Vardaman and Lerone Bennett Jr.—would agree that Lincoln was a racist. Nor is it surprising that others would suggest the point of view that could be labeled the Huck Finn theory: that Lincoln was a tortured and conflicted soul who waged a long and eventually successful battle to transcend his own inner bigotry.

Perhaps, but it seems unlikely. In light of the definitive evidence that Lincoln in the White House was a Machiavellian strategist—a strategist with moral objectives—a man who juxtaposed deception and persuasion, the ambiguous (or at least the more nuanced) evidence suggesting that Lincoln used the very same methods in the 1850s is overpowering. Even if the Huck Finn theory is supposed for the sake of the argument, a great many facts about Lincoln's behavior in the 1850s seem confusing. But if the master-politician theory is supposed, then the pieces fit together—if not with the precision of the fabled Swiss watch, then at least enough to justify the theory as the best hypothesis.

Both Stephen Douglas and Frederick Douglass would seem to have been right about Lincoln, from their opposite (to say the least) perspectives. It would seem as if Lincoln was a secret "negro lover," just as Stephen Douglas warned, and Frederick Douglass (at least in 1865) rejoiced: "the black man's president."

Why doubt the word of someone like Douglass, who relates that Lincoln's face "lighted up" when his own arrival was announced—and who put him so completely at ease that all sense of race identity vanished? What motive would have Douglass had to lie? We have to remember that the meetings of Douglass and Lincoln were observed—in the presidential office, at the second inaugural ball, and on other occasions, so that Douglass, if he made things up, could have been exposed and especially after his public eulogy of Lincoln in 1865.

No, there is no good reason to impeach the reminiscences of Douglass—except for the words that Douglass spoke a decade later. On April 14, 1876, he gave a speech about Lincoln in Washington, D.C., where a statue of Lincoln was being unveiled on Capitol Hill. In this speech, the warm enthusiasm of 1865 had cooled. Indeed, the Frederick Douglass who had called Lincoln "emphatically the black man's president" in 1865 now spoke of him as "preeminently the white man's president." Douglass said that it was whites who were "the children of Abraham Lincoln. We are at best only his stepchildren; children by adoption, children by forces of circumstances and necessity."[1]

Lincoln, said Douglass, "was ready and willing at any time during the first years of his administration to deny, postpone, and sacrifice the rights of humanity in the colored people to promote the welfare of the white people of this country." But then Douglass returned to his earlier views about the mitigating circumstances of strategy. After repeating that "Lincoln was a white man, and shared the prejudices common to his countrymen toward the colored race," Douglass added the following observations:

> Looking back to his times and to the condition of his country, we are compelled to admit that this unfriendly feeling on his part may be safely set down as one element of his wonderful success in organizing the loyal American people for the tremendous conflict before them, and bringing them safely through that conflict. His great mission was to accomplish two things: first, to save his country from dismemberment and ruin; and, second, to free his country from the great crime of slavery. To

do one or the other, or both, he must have the earnest sympathy and the powerful cooperation of his loyal fellow-countrymen. Without this primary and essential condition to success his efforts must have been vain and utterly fruitless.

In other lines that are frequently quoted, Douglass made this telling comparison: "Viewed from the genuine abolition ground, Mr. Lincoln seemed tardy, cold, dull, and indifferent; but measuring him by the sentiment of his country, a sentiment he was bound as a statesman to consult, he was swift, zealous, radical, and determined."[2]

Yet, the contrast between the two assessments of Lincoln by Douglass is stunning: from the man who was "emphatically the black man's president" in 1865 to the man who was "preeminently the white man's president"—from the man with whom Douglass "was never in any way reminded of my humble origin or of my unpopular color" to the man who "shared the prejudices common to his countrymen toward the colored race" and displayed an "unfriendly feeling"—we are left to wonder what happened to the feelings of Douglass in regard to Lincoln. Though much of his 1865 eulogy was repeated in the 1876 oration, something had changed. What could prompt such profound second thoughts?

Perhaps the force of extraneous factors? Perhaps a bitterness in Douglass (conscious or unconscious) as he watched Reconstruction sputter out? Perhaps a sense of disillusionment as the Gilded Age started and so many of the freedmen were betrayed? If so, Douglass kept such feelings suppressed, for his 1876 oration was triumphal in its tone.

Perhaps it came down to the belief of Douglass that a man of great honor like Abraham Lincoln would never—ever—tell a lie. Here are Douglass's pronouncements on the character of Abraham Lincoln:

- "He was a mystery to no man who saw him and heard him."
- "Though deep, he was transparent."
- "The image of the man went out with his words, and those who read them knew him."
- "His moral training was against his saying one thing when he meant another."[3]

Maybe here is the answer: Douglass was averse to confronting the fact that Lincoln sometimes practiced deception. Any man of great honor, by Douglass's standards, would be fearless, outspoken, and defiant (like Douglass himself), never tricky. So if Lincoln had declared that his "feelings would not admit" political and social equality for blacks (as he said in 1854), then he must have been sincere when he said it, Douglass probably reasoned. He must have shared the conventional prejudice and then . . . overcome it.

But Douglass got it right the first time in his 1865 eulogy. The behavior of Lincoln that Douglass would ascribe later on to "unfriendly feeling"—a "feeling" he had never experienced in person when he called upon Lincoln—was the behavior of the very same man who confided to some that he could spike the political soda "unbeknownst to himself." He would outmaneuver the racists. When Lincoln said the sort of things that racists expected to hear, he was . . . maneuvering.

Exceptional people come along sometimes, and to know them—to know Lincoln—one must analyze the evidence in all its complexity and then use the force of intuition. And so the following conjecture may be offered: Lincoln was free of any gut-level bias. There was no racial malice in his soul.

ACKNOWLEDGMENTS

I thank Sylvia Frank Rodrigue, Sara Gabbard, Richard Wayne Etulain, and William Pederson for their support and invaluable suggestions. Any errors in the book are my own.

Preface

1. Barzun, *From Dawn to Decadence*, 577–78, 694–95.
2. Riley, *Beneath the Mask*, 128.

Introduction

1. See Current, *Lincoln Nobody Knows*, 231–33, for commentary on Vardaman's allegations regarding Lincoln.
2. Bennett, *Forced into Glory*. See also Bennett's earlier article "Was Abe Lincoln a White Supremacist?"
3. See Quarles, *Lincoln and the Negro*; Strickland, "Illinois Background of Lincoln's Attitude"; Cain, "Lincoln's Views on Slavery and the Negro"; Fehrenbacher, "Only His Stepchildren"; Fredrickson, "Man, but Not a Brother"; Zilversmit, "Lincoln and the Problem of Race"; L. Cox, *Lincoln and Black Freedom*; Dirck, *Lincoln Emancipated*; Fredrickson, *Big Enough to Be Inconsistent*; and Krannawitter, *Vindicating Lincoln*.
4. For previous expositions of the author's views on this subject, see Striner, *Father Abraham*, and Striner, "Lincoln, Race, and Moral Strategy."

1. Lincoln, Slavery, and Race: The Problems

1. Burlingame, *Abraham Lincoln*, 1:67–71.
2. Abraham Lincoln to Mary Speed, September 27, 1841, in Basler, *Collected Works of Abraham Lincoln*, 1:260, and Abraham Lincoln to Joshua Speed, August 24, 1855, ibid., 2:320.
3. W. L. Miller, *Lincoln's Virtues*, 117, 346. See also Berwanger, *Frontier against Slavery*, 49; Voegeli, *Free but Not Equal*; and Litwack, *North of Slavery*.
4. Stampp, *Peculiar Institution*, 211, and Franklin, *Militant South*.
5. On the use of slaves as strikebreakers, see Genovese, *Political Economy of Slavery*, 199, 233, and Starobin, *Industrial Slavery in the Old South*. For coverage of the Tredegar strike, see Stampp, *Peculiar Institution*, 65, 426.
6. Fitzhugh, *Sociology for the South*, 179.
7. Quarles, *Black Abolitionists*, 3–4.
8. Berlin, *Slaves without Masters*, 356–57.
9. William Lloyd Garrison, quoted in Nye, *William Lloyd Garrison and the Humanitarian Reformers*, 22, 68.
10. James Hamilton Jr. to John Taylor et al., September 14, 1830, *Charleston (SC) Mercury*, cited in Freehling, *Prelude to Civil War*, 256.
11. Abraham Lincoln, "Eulogy on Henry Clay," July 6, 1852, in Basler, *Collected Works*, 2:132. For commentary on the issue of Lincoln's views

regarding colonization, see Scheips, "Lincoln and the Chiriqui Colonization Project"; Vorenberg, "Abraham Lincoln and the Politics of Black Colonization," 22–45; Freehling, "'Absurd' Issues and the Causes of the Civil War: Colonization as a Test Case," 138–57; Boritt, "Did He Dream of a Lily-White America?" and Paludan, "Lincoln and Colonization."

2. The 1854 Peoria Speech and Its Context

1. Lincoln, "Speech at Peoria, Illinois," October 16, 1854, in Basler, *Collected Works*, 2:281.
2. Ibid., 264.
3. Ibid., 265.
4. Ibid., 265, 266.
5. See Gould, *Mismeasure of Man*; Stanton, *Leopard's Spots*; and Lurie, "Louis Agassiz and the Races of Man."
6. Nott and Glidden, *Types of Mankind*.
7. Van Evrie, *Negroes and Negro "Slavery,"* v.
8. Van Evrie, cited in Lander, *Lincoln & Darwin*, 172.
9. Lincoln, "Speech at Peoria, Illinois," in Basler, *Collected Works*, 2:275, 271.
10. Ibid., 255–56.
11. Jaffa, *Crisis of the House Divided*, 383.
12. David Grimsted, letter to author, January 31, 2002.
13. Lincoln, "Fragment on Slavery," ca. July 1, 1854, in Basler, *Collected Works*, 2:222–23.

3. The 1857 Springfield Speech and Its Context

1. Lincoln, "Speech at Springfield, Illinois," June 26, 1857, in Basler, *Collected Works*, 2:404.
2. Ibid., 405–6.
3. Ibid.
4. Ibid.
5. Thomas Jefferson to the Reverend Charles Clay, January 27, 1790, in Boyd, *Papers of Thomas Jefferson*, 16:129.
6. Lincoln, "Speech at Springfield," in Basler, *Collected Works*, 2:405. Lincoln deftly pointed out that the "near-universal disgust" among whites in regard to race mixing was in no way *completely* universal, and his proof of this fact was . . . mulattoes. In the course of the Springfield speech, he referred to women slaves who were "mothers of mulattoes in spite of themselves" through "forced concubinage," thus proving the hypocrisy among white males, in the slave states at least, in regard to their public professions of "disgust" in regard to "race mixing." Ibid., 2:408–9.
7. Ibid., 407.

8. Ibid., 408.

9. Owen Lovejoy, Speech of February 1859, in Moore and Moore, *His Brother's Blood*, 177.

10. Henry Wilson, Cong. Globe, 36th Cong., 1st Sess., April 12, 1860, (1685).

11. William H. Seward, "The National Divergence and Return," speech, September 4, 1860, in Baker, *Works of William Henry Seward*, 4:317.

12. Stephen A. Douglas, "Senator Douglas's Reply," in "Sixth Debate with Stephen A. Douglas at Quincy, Illinois, October 13, 1858," in Basler, *Collected Works*, 3:261.

4. The Lincoln-Douglas Debates

1. Abraham Lincoln, "Speech at Chicago," July 10, 1858, in Basler, *Collected Works*, 2:500–501.

2. Stephen Douglas, speech at Chicago, July 9, 1858, quoted in Burlingame, *Abraham Lincoln*, 1:467–68.

3. Stephen Douglas, speech at Springfield, Illinois, July 17, 1858, quoted in ibid., 474.

4. Stephen Douglas, speech at Bloomington, Illinois, July 16, 1858, quoted in ibid., 473.

5. Stephen Douglas, speech at Springfield, Illinois, July 17, 1858, quoted in ibid., 474.

6. Abraham Lincoln, "Speech at Springfield, Illinois," July 17, 1858, in Basler, *Collected Works*, 2:519–20.

7. Abraham Lincoln, "Fragment on Pro-Slavery Theology," ca. October 1, 1858, ibid., 3:204.

8. Bellow, *Mr. Sammler's Planet*, 286.

9. Stephen Douglas, "Mr. Douglas's Speech," in "First Debate with Stephen A. Douglas at Ottawa, Illinois," August 21, 1858, in Basler, *Collected Works*, 3:9.

10. Ibid., 3:10.

11. Stephen Douglas, "Mr. Douglas's Speech," in "Second Debate with Stephen A. Douglas at Freeport, Illinois," August 27, 1858, in ibid., 3:55–56.

12. Stephen Douglas, "Mr. Douglas's Speech," in "Third Debate with Stephen A. Douglas at Jonesboro, Illinois," September 15, 1858, in ibid., 3:105, 113.

13. Lincoln, "Mr. Lincoln's Speech," in "Fourth Debate with Stephen A. Douglas at Charleston, Illinois," September 18, 1858, in ibid., 3:146.

14. Lincoln, "Mr. Lincoln's Reply," in "First Debate with Stephen A. Douglas at Ottawa, Illinois," August 21, 1858, in ibid., 3:16.

15. Abraham Lincoln, "Speech at Hartford, Connecticut," March 5, 1860, in ibid., 4:10.

5. The 1859 Columbus Speech

1. Stephen Douglas, speech in Memphis, Tennessee, November 30, 1858, quoted in *Chicago Times*, December 8, 1858.
2. Lincoln, "Notes for Speeches at Columbus and Cincinnati, Ohio," September 16, 17, 1859, in Basler, *Collected Works of Abraham Lincoln*, 3:431–32.
3. Lincoln, "Speech at Columbus, Ohio," September 16, 1859, in ibid., 3:423.
4. Ibid., 3:423–24.
5. Ibid., 3:424.
6. David R. Locke, quoted in Rice, *Reminiscences of Abraham Lincoln*, 446–47.

6. Emancipation, Colonization, and the Equal Rights Possibility

1. Alexander Stephens, speech at Savannah, March 21, 1861, in Stampp, *Causes of the Civil War*, 116.
2. Mosse, *Crisis of German Ideology*.
3. See Bonner, "Slavery, Confederate Diplomacy, and the Racialist Mission of Henry Hotze."
4. Owen, "Gorilla and the Negro," 395–96.
5. See Hunt, *Negro's Place in Nature*.
6. For Darwin's views on slavery and race, see Lander, *Lincoln & Darwin*.
7. Lincoln, "Drafts for a Bill for Compensated Emancipation in Delaware," ca. November 26, 1861, in Basler, *Collected Works*, 5:29–30.
8. Conway, *Autobiography, Memories, and Experiences*, 1:345–46.
9. According to LaWanda Cox, Phillips wrote about a story Lincoln told him concerning "an Irishman in legally dry Maine who asked for a glass of soda with 'a drop of the crathur [put] into it *unbeknown to myself.*'" See L. Cox, *Lincoln and Black Freedom*, 8.
10. Abraham Lincoln to Horace Greeley, August 22, 1862, in Basler, *Collected Works*, 5:388–89.
11. Julian, *Speeches of Political Questions*, 127. See Voegeli, *Free but Not Equal*, 6; Wood, *Black Scare*, 35; and Klement, *Copperheads in the Middle West*, 14.
12. John Palmer Usher, quoted in Burlingame, *Abraham Lincoln*, 2:383.
13. "Report of the Select Committee on Emancipation and Colonization," 14–16.
14. Abraham Lincoln, "Address on Colonization to a Deputation of Negroes," August 14, 1862, in Basler, *Collected Works*, 5:370–75. For an account of the Chiriqui project, see ibid., 370–71n1; Scheips, "Lincoln and the Chiriqui Colonization Project"; and Burlingame, *Abraham Lincoln*, 2:387–95.

15. Burlingame, *Abraham Lincoln*, 2:389, 390.

16. Ibid., 2:393, 394.

17. Ibid., 2:395–96.

18. Lincoln, "Annual Message to Congress," December 1, 1862, in Basler, *Collected Works*, 5:535.

19. Ibid., 5:537.

20. Abraham Lincoln to Andrew Johnson, March 26, 1863, in Basler, *Collected Works*, 6:149–50.

21. Abraham Lincoln to James C. Conkling, August 26, 1863, in ibid., 6:406–10.

22. Douglass, *Life and Times of Frederick Douglass*, 430.

23. Ibid., 421.

24. Ibid., 422.

25. Ibid. 422, 436.

26. Ibid., 422–23.

27. Ibid., 423.

28. Abraham Lincoln, "Instructions to Tax Commissioners in South Carolina," September 16, 1863, in Basler, *Collected Works*, 6:457.

29. Abraham Lincoln to Stephen A. Hurlbut, ca. August 15, 1863, ibid., 6:387.

30. Abraham Lincoln, "Fragment," circa August 26, 1863, ibid., 6:410–11.

7. Voting Rights and Lincoln's Murder

1. Lincoln to E. E. Malhiot, Bradish Johnson, and Thomas Cottman, June 19, 1863, in Basler, *Collected Works*, 6:288.

2. Lincoln to Nathaniel Banks, August 5, 1863, in ibid., 6:364–65.

3. Lincoln to Andrew Johnson, September 11, 1863, in ibid., 6:440.

4. Foner, *Short History of Reconstruction*, 21.

5. Lincoln to Michael Hahn, March 13, 1864, in Basler, *Collected Works*, 7:243.

6. See Keyssar, *Right to Vote*, 142.

7. L. Cox, *Lincoln and Black Freedom*, 18. See also Vorenberg, *Final Freedom*.

8. McPherson, *Ordeal by Fire*, 467.

9. Quarles, *Lincoln and the Negro*, 233.

10. See Kaplan, "Miscegenation Issue in the Election of 1864."

11. Editorial, *Columbus (OH) Crisis*, August 3, 1864, and *Freeman's Journal*, August 20, 1864, quoted in McPherson, *Ordeal by Fire*, 438, 449; Wood, *Black Scare*, 53–79.

12. Vorenberg, *Final Freedom*, 160–63.

13. "Miscegenation Ball."

14. John Nicolay to John McMahon, August 6, 1864, in Basler, *Collected Works*, 7:483.

15. Douglass, *Life and Times of Frederick Douglass*, 434–35.

16. James M. McPherson, "The Ballot and Land for the Freedmen, 1861–1865," in Stampp and Litwack, *Reconstruction*, 152–53.
17. Douglass, *Life and Times of Frederick Douglass*, 444–45. See also Oakes, *Radical and the Republican*, 242.
18. Quarles, *Lincoln and the Negro*, 235.
19. Ibid., 235–36.
20. Lincoln, "Last Public Address," April 11, 1865, in Basler, *Collected Works*, 8:399–405.
21. Ibid.
22. Hanchett, *Lincoln Murder Conspiracies*, 37, and Steers, *Blood on the Moon*, 91.
23. Burlingame, *Abraham Lincoln*, 2:811.
24. "Agate," in *Cincinnati Gazette*, July 23, 1865, quoted in Hyman, "Lincoln and Equal Rights for Negroes, 265–66.
25. Conway, *Autobiography, Memories, and Experiences*, 2:206.
26. Salmon Chase to Abraham Lincoln, April 12, 1865, in Schuckers, *Life and Public Services of Salmon Portland Chase*, 516–18.
27. "Agate" [Whitelaw Reid], quoted in Hyman, "Lincoln and Equal Rights for Negroes," 255–56.
28. Frederick Douglass, quoted in Burlingame, *Abraham Lincoln*, 2:829–31. On the meeting with Lincoln during which a governor (the governor of Connecticut) had to wait because the president was in conversation with Douglass, see Oakes, *Radical and the Republican*, 232.

8. Disputed or Doubtful Evidence

1. For commentary on this matter, see Johnson, "Lincoln and Equal Rights," and Hyman, "Lincoln and Equal Rights for Negroes."
2. Lamon, *Recollections of Abraham Lincoln*, 242.
3. Lincoln, "Reply to Emancipation Memorial Presented by Chicago Christians of All Denominations," September 13, 1862, in Basler, *Collected Works*, 5:420–25.
4. Butler, *Autobiography*, 903–4, and Rice, *Reminiscences of Abraham Lincoln*, 259–60.
5. Neely, "Abraham Lincoln and Black Colonization," 77–83.
6. Magness, "Benjamin Butler's Colonization Testimony Reevaluated," 1–28.
7. Butler, *Autobiography*, 903.

9. Lincoln and Native Americans

1. For accounts of this war, see Oehler, *Great Sioux Uprising*; D. Miller, "Lincoln and the Sioux Outbreak"; Anderson, *Little Crow*; Schultz, *Over the Earth I Come;* Keenan, *Great Sioux Uprising*; and H. H. Cox, *Lincoln and the Sioux Uprising of 1862.*

2. See Kelsey, "Abraham Lincoln and American Indian Policy"; Nichols, *Lincoln and the Indians*; and Etulain, *Lincoln Looks West*.

3. See Moulton, *John Ross*, 174–76, and Prucha, *Great Father*, 1:419–27.

4. John Ross to Lincoln, September 16, 1862, in Moulton, *Papers of Chief John Ross*, 2:516–18.

5. Lincoln to John Ross, September 25, 1862, in Basler, *Collected Works*, 5:439–40.

6. Prucha, *Great Father*, 427.

7. *Washington (DC) Daily Morning Chronicle*, March 28, 1863, in Basler, *Collected Works*, 6:152–53 n1.

8. Lincoln, Speech to Indians, March 27, 1863, in ibid., 6:151–52.

10. Racist or Not?

1. Douglass, "Oration in Memory of Abraham Lincoln, Delivered at the Unveiling of the Freedmen's Monument in Memory of Abraham Lincoln in Lincoln Park, Washington, DC, April 14, 1876," *Life and Writings*, 4:312. See also Oakes, *Radical and the Republican*.

2. Douglass, "Oration in Memory of Abraham Lincoln," *Life and Writings*, 4:312, 315, 315–16, 316.

3. Ibid., 4:315, 318.

BIBLIOGRAPHY

Anderson, Gary Clayton. *Little Crow: Spokesman for the Sioux*. St. Paul: Minnesota Historical Society Press, 1986.

Baker, George E., ed. *The Works of William Henry Seward*. 5 vols. Boston: Houghton Mifflin, 1884–87.

Barzun, Jacques. *From Dawn to Decadence: 500 Years of Western Cultural Life*. Perennial ed. New York: HarperCollins, 2000.

———. *Race: A Study in Modern Superstition*. New York: Harcourt, Brace, 1937.

Basler, Roy P., et al., eds. *The Collected Works of Abraham Lincoln*. 9 vols. New Brunswick, NJ: Rutgers University Press, 1953–55.

Bellow, Saul. *Mr. Sammler's Planet*. Paper ed. New York: Fawcett, 1970. First published in 1969 by Viking. Citations refer to the Fawcett edition.

Bennett, Lerone, Jr. *Forced into Glory: Abraham Lincoln's White Dream*. Chicago: Johnson, 2000.

———. "Was Abe Lincoln a White Supremacist?" *Ebony*, February 1968, 35–38.

Berlin, Ira. *Slaves without Masters: The Free Negro in the Antebellum South*. New York: Oxford University Press, 1974.

Berwanger, Eugene H. *The Frontier against Slavery: Western Anti-Negro Prejudice and the Slavery Extension Controversy*. Urbana: University of Illinois Press, 1967.

Bonner, Robert E. "Slavery, Confederate Diplomacy, and the Racialist Mission of Henry Hotze." *Civil War History* 51 (2005): 288–316.

Boritt, Gabor. "Did He Dream of a Lily-White America? The Voyage to Lincolnia." In *The Lincoln Enigma: The Changing Face of an American Icon*, edited by Boritt, 1–19. New York: Oxford University Press, 2001.

Boyd, Julian P., et al., eds. *The Papers of Thomas Jefferson*. Princeton: Princeton University Press, 1950–.

Burlingame, Michael. *Abraham Lincoln: A Life*. 2 vols. Baltimore: Johns Hopkins University Press, 2008.

Butler, Benjamin F. *Autobiography and Personal Reminiscences of Major General Benjamin F. Butler*. Boston: A. M. Thayer, 1892.

Cain, Marvin R. "Lincoln's Views on Slavery and the Negro: A Suggestion." *Historian* 26 (1964): 502–20.

Conway, Moncure Daniel. *Autobiography, Memories, and Experiences*. New York: Houghton Mifflin, 1904.

Cox, Hank H. *Lincoln and the Sioux Uprising of 1862*. Nashville, TN: Cumberland, 2005.

Cox, LaWanda. *Lincoln and Black Freedom: A Study in Presidential Leadership*. Columbia: University of South Carolina Press, 1981.

Current, Richard N. *The Lincoln Nobody Knows*. New York: Hill & Wang, 1958.

Dirck, Brian R., ed. *Lincoln Emancipated: The President and the Politics of Race*. DeKalb: Northern Illinois University Press, 2007.

Donald, David Herbert. *Lincoln Reconsidered: Essays on the Civil War Era*. New York: Knopf, 1956.

Douglass, Frederick. *Life and Times of Frederick Douglass, Written by Himself*. Hartford, CT: Park, 1882.

———. *The Life and Writings of Frederick Douglass*. Edited by Philip S. Foner. New York: International, 1955.

Etulain, Richard W. *Lincoln Looks West: From the Mississippi to the Pacific*. Carbondale: Southern Illinois University Press, 2010.

Fehrenbacher, Don E. "Only His Stepchildren: Lincoln and the Negro." *Civil War History* 20 (December 1974): 293–310.

Fitzhugh, George. *Sociology for the South—or, the Failure of Free Society*. Burt Franklin Research and Source Book Series 102. Richmond: A. Morris, 1854.

Foner, Eric. *The Fiery Trial: Abraham Lincoln and American Slavery*. New York: Norton, 2010.

———. *Short History of Reconstruction, 1863–1877*. New York: Harper & Row, 1990.

Franklin, John Hope. *The Militant South, 1800–1861*. Cambridge: Harvard University Press, 1956.

Fredrickson, George M. *Big Enough to Be Inconsistent: Abraham Lincoln Confronts Slavery and Race*. Cambridge: Harvard University Press, 2008.

———. "A Man, but Not a Brother: Abraham Lincoln and Racial Equality." *Journal of Southern History* 41 (February 1975): 39–58.

Freehling, William W. "'Absurd' Issues and the Causes of the Civil War: Colonization as a Test Case." In *The Reintegration of American History: Slavery and the Civil War*, 138–57. New York: Oxford University Press, 1994.

———. *Prelude to Civil War: The Nullification Controversy in South Carolina, 1816–1836*. New York: Harper & Row, 1965.

Genovese, Eugene D. *The Political Economy of Slavery*. New York: Random, 1965.

Gould, Stephen Jay. *The Mismeasure of Man*. New York: Norton, 1981.

Guelzo, Allen C. "Foreword—Was Lincoln a Racist?" In Dirck, *Lincoln Emancipated*, vii–xiv.

Hanchett, William. *The Lincoln Murder Conspiracies*. Urbana: University of Illinois Press, 1983.

Hofstadter, Richard. *The American Political Tradition and the Men Who Made It*. New York: Knopf, 1948.

Hunt, James. *The Negro's Place in Nature.* London: Trübner, 1863.

Hyman, Harold M. "Lincoln and Equal Rights for Negroes: The Irrelevancy of the 'Wadsworth Letter.'" *Civil War History* 12 (September 1966): 265–66.

Jaffa, Harry V. *Crisis of the House Divided: An Interpretation of the Lincoln-Douglas Debates.* Chicago: University of Chicago Press, 1959.

Johnson, Ludwell H. "Lincoln and Equal Rights: The Authenticity of the Wadsworth Letter." *Journal of Southern History* 32 (February 1966): 83–87.

Julian, George Washington. *Speeches on Political Questions.* New York: Hurd & Houghton, 1872.

Kaplan, Sidney. "The Miscegenation Issue in the Election of 1864." *Journal of Negro History* 34 (1949): 274–343.

Keenan, Jerry. *The Great Sioux Uprising.* New York: Da Capo, 2003.

Kelsey, Harry. "Abraham Lincoln and American Indian Policy." *Lincoln Herald* 77 (Fall 1975): 139–48.

Keyssar, Alexander. *The Right to Vote: The Contested History of Democracy in the United States.* New York: Basic Books, 2000.

Klement, Frank L. *The Copperheads in the Middle West.* Chicago: University of Chicago Press, 1960.

Krannawitter, Thomas L. *Vindicating Lincoln: Defending the Politics of Our Greatest President.* Lanham, MD: Rowman & Littlefield, 2008.

Lamon, Ward Hill. *Recollections of Abraham Lincoln, 1847–1865.* Edited by Dorothy Lamon Teillard. Washington, DC: Lamon Teillard, 1911.

Lander, James. *Lincoln & Darwin: The Shared Vision of Race, Science, and Religion.* Carbondale: Southern Illinois University Press, 2010.

Lincoln, Abraham. *The Collected Works of Abraham Lincoln.* Edited by Roy P. Basler. 9 vols. New Brunswick, NJ: Rutgers University Press, 1953–55.

Litwack, Leon F. *North of Slavery: The Negro in the Free States, 1790–1860.* Chicago: University of Chicago Press, 1961.

Lurie, Edward. "Louis Agassiz and the Races of Man." *Isis* 45 (September 1954): 227–42.

Magness, Philip W. "Benjamin Butler's Colonization Testimony Reevaluated." *Journal of the Abraham Lincoln Association* 29 (2008): 1–28.

McPherson, James M. "The Ballot and Land for the Freedmen, 1861–1865." In *Reconstruction: An Anthology of Revisionist Writings,* edited by Kenneth Stampp and Leon F. Litwack. Baton Rouge: Louisiana State University Press, 1969, 152–53.

———. *Ordeal by Fire: The Civil War and Reconstruction.* 1982. New York: McGraw-Hill, 1992. Citations refer to the 1992 edition.

Miller, David. "Lincoln and the Sioux Outbreak." In *Lincoln: A Contemporary Portrait,* edited by Allan Nevins and Irving Stone. Garden City, NJ: Doubleday, 1962, 111–30.

Miller, William Lee. *Lincoln's Virtues: An Ethical Biography*. New York: Knopf, 2002.

"Miscegenation Ball, The." Political caricature, no. 4. G. W. Bromley, 1864. LC-USZ62-14828, Prints and Photographs Division, Library of Congress.

Moore, William F., and Jane Ann Moore, eds. *His Brother's Blood: Owen Lovejoy, Speeches and Writings, 1838–1864*. Urbana: University of Illinois Press, 2004.

Mosse, George L. *The Crisis of German Ideology: Intellectual Origins of the Third Reich*. New York: Grosset & Dunlap, 1964.

Moulton, Gary E. *John Ross, Cherokee Chief*. Athens: University of Georgia Press, 1978.

———. *The Papers of Chief John Ross*. 2 vols. Norman: University of Oklahoma Press, 1985.

Neely, Mark E. "Abraham Lincoln and Black Colonization: Benjamin Butler's Spurious Testimony." *Civil War History* 25 (1979): 77–83.

Nichols, David A. *Lincoln and the Indians: Civil War Policy and Politics*. Columbia: University of Missouri Press, 1978.

Nott, Josiah Clark, and George Robins Glidden. *Types of Mankind: Or, Ethnological Researches, Based upon the Ancient Monuments, Paintings, Sculptures, and Crania of Races*. Philadelphia: Lippincott, Grambo, 1854.

Nye, Russel B. *William Lloyd Garrison and the Humanitarian Reformers*. Boston: Little, Brown, 1955.

Oakes, James. "Natural Rights, Citizenship Rights, States' Rights, and Black Rights: Another Look at Lincoln and Race." In *Our Lincoln: New Perspectives on Lincoln and His World*, edited by Eric Foner. New York: Norton, 2008. 109–34.

———. *The Radical and the Republican: Frederick Douglass, Abraham Lincoln, and the Triumph of Antislavery Politics*. New York: Norton, 2007.

Oehler, C. M. *The Great Sioux Uprising*. New York: Oxford University Press, 1959.

Owen, Richard. "The Gorilla and the Negro." *Athenaeum* 1743 (March 23, 1861): 395–96.

Paludan, Philip Shaw. "Greeley, Colonization, and a 'Deputation of Negroes.'" In Dirck, *Lincoln Emancipated*, 29–46.

———. "Lincoln and Colonization: Policy or Propaganda?" *Journal of the Abraham Lincoln Association* 25 (2004): 23–37.

Prucha, Francis Paul. *The Great Father: The United States Government and the American Indians*. Lincoln: University of Nebraska Press, 1984.

Quarles, Benjamin. *Black Abolitionists*. 1969. New York: Oxford University Press, 1970. Citations refer to the 1970 edition.

———. *Lincoln and the Negro*. New York: Oxford University Press, 1962.

"Report of the Select Committee on Emancipation and Colonization." House Reports no. 148, 37th Cong., 2nd Sess., July 16, 1862. Washington, DC: GPO, 1862.

Rice, Allen Thorndike. ed. *Reminiscences of Abraham Lincoln by Distinguished Men of His Time*. New York: North American Review, 1886.

Riley, Debbie. *Beneath the Mask: Understanding Adopted Teens, Case Studies and Treatment Considerations for Therapists and Parents*. With John Meeks. Silver Spring, MD: Center for Adoption Support and Education, 2006.

Scheips, Paul J. "Lincoln and the Chiriqui Colonization Project." *Journal of Negro History* 37 (October 1952): 418–53.

Schuckers, Jacob W. *The Life and Public Services of Salmon Portland Chase*. New York: Appleton, 1874.

Schultz, Duane. *Over the Earth I Come: The Great Sioux Uprising of 1862*. New York: St. Martin's, 1992.

Stampp, Kenneth M., ed. *The Causes of the Civil War*. 1959. Englewood Cliffs, NJ: Prentice Hall, 1974. Citations refer to the 1974 edition.

———. *The Peculiar Institution: Slavery in the Antebellum South*. New York: Knopf, 1956.

Stampp, Kenneth, and Leon F. Litwack, eds. *Reconstruction: An Anthology of Revisionist Writings*. Baton Rouge: Louisiana State University Press, 1969.

Stanton, William. *The Leopard's Spots: Scientific Attitudes toward Race in America, 1815–59*. Chicago: University of Chicago Press, 1960.

Starobin, Robert S. *Industrial Slavery in the Old South*. New York: Oxford University Press, 1970.

Steers, Edward, Jr. *Blood on the Moon: The Assassination of Abraham Lincoln*. Lexington: University Press of Kentucky, 2001.

Strickland, Arvah E. "The Illinois Background of Lincoln's Attitude toward Slavery and the Negro." *Illinois State Historical Society Journal* 56 (Autumn 1963): 474–94.

Striner, Richard. *Father Abraham: Lincoln's Relentless Struggle to End Slavery*. New York: Oxford University Press, 2006.

———. "Lincoln, Race, and Moral Strategy." *Lincoln Lore*, Winter 2008, 6–11.

Van Evrie, John H. *Negroes and Negro "Slavery": The First an Inferior Race; the Latter Its Normal Condition*. New York: Van Evrie, Horton, 1861.

Voegeli, Jacques. *Free but Not Equal: The Midwest and the Negro during the Civil War*. Chicago: University of Chicago Press, 1967.

Vorenberg, Michael. "Abraham Lincoln and the Politics of Black Colonization." *Journal of the Abraham Lincoln Association* 14 (Summer 1993): 22–45.

———. *Final Freedom: The Civil War, the Abolition of Slavery, and the Thirteenth Amendment*. Cambridge: Cambridge University Press, 2001.

Winkle, Kenneth J. "Paradox Though It May Seem: Lincoln on Antislavery, Race, and Union." In Dirck, *Lincoln Emancipated*, 8–28.

Wood, Forrest G. *Black Scare: The Racist Response to Emancipation and Reconstruction*. Berkeley: University of California Press, 1968.

Zilversmit, Arthur. "Lincoln and the Problem of Race: A Decade of Interpretations." *Papers of the Abraham Lincoln Association* 2 (Summer 1980): 21–44.

INDEX

Agassiz, Louis, 10
American Colonization Society, 6

Banks, Nathaniel, 50–51, 57
Barzun, Jacques, x
Bennett, Lerone, Jr., 1, 29, 70
Berlin, Ira, 6
Bertonneau, Arnold, 52
Blackhawk War, 3
Booth, John Wilkes, 58
Burlingame, Michael, 58
Butler, Benjamin, 62–63

Channing, William Ellery, 37–38
Chase, Salmon, 58
Chiriqui project, 41–42
civil war politics, 35–60, 47–48,
    53–54
Clay, Henry, 6
colonization, 6–7, 11, 40–43, 53,
    62–63
Confederate States of America,
    36–37, 47
Conkling, James C., 44
constitutional amendments, 48, 49,
    52, 53, 55
Conway, Moncure Daniel, 37–38, 58

Darwin, Charles, 37
Declaration of Independence, 15–17,
    21–23, 33
Democratic Party politics, 8, 14, 31,
    35, 39, 53–54
Douglas, Stephen A., 1, 8–12, 14–20,
    21–30, 31–34, 37, 70
Douglass, Frederick, 42, 45–46, 53,
    55, 56, 59–60, 70–73
Dred Scott decision, 14–16, 21

Emancipation Proclamation, 39–40,
    43, 48
equality, denotations and connota-
    tions of, 18–20, 24–25, 33

Fitzhugh, George, 5
Freedmen's Bureau, 56
free soil movement, 3–5, 8, 12

Garnet, Henry Highland, 42
Garrison, William Lloyd, 6
Goodman, David, 54
Grant, Ulysses S., 44, 54
Greeley, Horace, 38

Hahn, Michael, 49, 51–52, 57
Henry, Joseph, 42, 68
Hotze, Henry, 37
Hunt, James, 37
Hurlbut, Stephen, 47

Ile-a-Vache, 43, 53
Illinois, racial politics of, 4, 17–20,
    23–30

Jaffa, Harry V., 12
Jefferson, Thomas, 16–17
Johnson, Andrew, 44, 50, 56

Kansas-Nebraska Act, 8
Kock, Bernard, 43

Lamon, Ward Hill, 61–62
Land redistribution during Civil
    War, 46–47, 55–56
Lincoln, Abraham: and 1862 message
    to Congress, 43–44; and black
    voting rights, 48, 50, 52–53,
    56–58; and colonization, 7, 11,
    40–43, 53, 62–63; and Chicago
    speech of July 10, 1858, 21–23; and
    Columbus speech of Septem-
    ber 16, 1859, 31–34; and covert
    "free state" strategy in 1863 and
    1864, 49–52, 56–59; and Stephen
    Douglas, 8–9, 14–20, 21–30,
    31–34, 37, 70; and Frederick
    Douglass, 42, 45–46, 53, 55, 56,

Richard Striner is a writer, scholar, teacher, and civic activist. He served as a professor of history for thirty years at Washington College. The author of over a dozen books, he is also the author of numerous magazine and journal articles as well as public affairs commentaries and op-eds. His most recent book is *Summoned to Glory: The Audacious Life of Abraham Lincoln*. Striner's previous presidential books include *Woodrow Wilson and World War I: A Burden Too Great to Bear, Lincoln and Race, Lincoln's Way: How Six Great Presidents Created American Power*, and *Father Abraham: Lincoln's Relentless Struggle to End Slavery*. He contributed to the on-line *New York Times* "Disunion" series on the Civil War and has written two cover stories for the *American Scholar* magazine.

**CONCISE
LINCOLN
LIBRARY**

This series of concise books fills a need for short studies of the life, times, and legacy of President Abraham Lincoln. Each book gives readers the opportunity to quickly achieve basic knowledge of a Lincoln-related topic. These books bring fresh perspectives to well-known topics, investigate previously overlooked subjects, and explore in greater depth topics that have not yet received book-length treatment. For a complete list of titles, see www.conciselincolnlibrary.com.

Other Books in the Concise Lincoln Library